# nihongo notes 3

## understanding japanese usage

by
osamu mizutani
nobuko mizutani

The **Japan Times**, Ltd.

ISBN4-7890-0127-X

First edition: September 1980
Eighth printing: October 1986

Jacket design by Koji Detake


Published by The Japan Times, Ltd.
5-4, Shibaura 4-chome, Minato-ku, Tokyo 108, Japan




Printed in Japan

# FOREWORD

This book is a compilation of the seventy columns which appeared in *The Japan Times* from April 8, 1979 to August 3, 1980 under the title "Nihongo Notes." (The preceding 140 columns have been published as *Nihongo Notes 1* and *Nihongo Notes 2*.) We have also added a list of basic example sentences and explanations entitled "Guide for Avoidance of Common Mistakes" as a supplement to these columns.

In this volume, while continuing to explain the actual usage of various Japanese expressions, we have attempted to take up more specific situations and to provide more detailed explanations. The columns in this volume deal with such diverse aspects of Japanese usage as socially significant words and phrases, exchanges in professional situations, reserved-sounding speech, the speech of senior members towards younger members in a group, the speech of young people, and word play.

It is a great pleasure to be able to publish another volume of *Nihongo Notes*. We hope that you will enjoy reading it and find some help in understanding more about how Japanese use their language.

We would like to acknowledge the help of Janet Ashby who checked the English for these columns and offered valuable suggestions just as she did for the preceding two volumes.

August, 1980
Osamu and Nobuko Mizutani

# CONTENTS

## Note Concerning Romanization

The romanization used in this book (as well as in *An Introduction to Modern Japanese*) is based on the Hepburn system with the following modifications.

1.  When the same vowel occurs consecutively, the letter is repeated rather than using the "-" mark.

    ex. *Tookyoo* (instead of *Tōkyō*)

2.  The sound indicated by the hiragana ん is written with "*n*" regardless of what sound follows it.

    ex. *shinbun* (instead of shimbun)

    ex. *shinpai* (instead of shimpai)

The words connected with hyphens are pronounced as one unit.

    ex. *genki-desu*

    ex. *Soo-desu-ne*

# *Tonikaku*
## とにかく
### (Anyway)

Yesterday afternoon Mr. Lerner left the office on business. When he had finished it was almost four, and he thought he might as well go straight home without going back to the office. So he called Mr. Takada at the office to make sure that would be all right. Mr. Takada immediately started to explain that some urgent business had come up while Mr. Lerner was out and he wanted him to come back to the office. Mr. Lerner didn't understand him well because he spoke rapidly, so he asked him to repeat it. Mr. Takada seemed to be irritated and said

*Tonikaku ichido modotte-kite-kudasai.*
とにかく　いちど　もどってきてください。
(Anyway, please come back once.)

＊　　　＊　　　＊

*Tonikaku* is sometimes used in such sentences as

*Umaku itte-mo ikanakute-mo tonikaku oshi-rase-shimasu.*
(I'll let you know anyway whether it goes well or not.)

just as the English "anyway" is used.

But more often it is used when the speaker feels that he has discussed a matter well enough or thought about it long enough and he wants to stop discussing or thinking about it; Mr. Takada used it this way in the case mentioned above.

You will often hear people say after some discussion

> *Tonikaku yatte-mimashoo.*
> とにかく　やってみましょう。
> (Anyway I'll give it a try.)
> *Tonikaku yatte-mite-kudasai.*
> (Anyway please give it a try.)

It is used not only when stating a decision or urging someone to start an action, but also when expressing a judgment as in

> *Tonikaku sore-wa komarimasu.*
> (Anyway it won't do.)
> *Tonikaku kare-wa dame-da.*
> (Anyway he won't do.)

Thus, after spending some time in discussing a matter, when someone, usually an influential person, says *Tonikaku . . .*, then the people there regard it as a sign indicating that the discussion is to be ended.

A young son, asking his father to buy something for him and eagerly explaining why he needs it, will dread more than anything else the word

> *Tonikaku . . .*

uttered by his father; it is most likely that the word will be followed by such phrases as

> . . . *ima-wa dame-da.* (I can't buy it now.)

or

> . . . *kyoo-wa kore-de yamete-okoo.* (Let's discuss it some other time. — *lit.* We won't discuss it any more today.)

9

# *Mottainai*
## もったいない
### (Too good to waste)

Last Friday was a beautiful day. Mr. Lerner had lunch near his office with Miss Yoshida and afterward she suggested that they take a walk. Mr. Lerner was rather busy that afternoon, so he was wondering if he shouldn't go straight back to the office. Then Miss Yoshida said that such a nice day was

> *Mottainai.* もったいない。
> (Too good to waste.)

He had heard this expression a couple of weeks before; when he was about to leave the room with the light on his desk left on, Miss Yoshida asked him to turn it off, since

> *Denki-ga mottainai.*
> 電気が もったいない。
> (One shouldn't waste electricity.)

He could understand the expression when it was used about saving electricity, but he wondered how it could be used with the day.

\*　　　\*　　　\*

Dictionaries give several definitions for the word *mottainai*; the meaning of the word has changed with the times. But at present it usually means "it is a pity not to do justice to something." Leaving a light on when it is not being used is *mottainai* since you're not doing justice to the electricity. Spending one's time without doing much is *mottainai* since one is not doing justice to his time. In the same way, staying inside when the day is nice and warm is *mottainai* because you're not doing justice to it.

Middle-aged Japanese remember often being told not to waste things when they were children. It was regarded as very bad to waste things, especially food, before the war. Rice was regarded as the most important food, and children were sometimes told to pick up even a grain of rice that had spilled on the ground because it was *mottainai* to waste it.

Although Japan's economic conditions have rapidly changed since the war, and children are not told to pick up spilled rice grains any more, this expression *mottainai* is still alive and used in various ways.

When something is too good for a specific purpose, it is also described as *mottainai*. When a generous mother buys an expensive student-bag for her son, her husband may criticize her by saying

*Gakusee-niwa mottainai.*
(Too good for a student.)

# *Aite*

## 相手

### (Companion)

During lunch time a few weeks ago someone started teasing Miss Yoshida and said that he didn't understand why such an attractive woman still remained single. Miss Yoshida laughed and said

> *Aite-ga imasen-kara-ne.*
> 相手が　いませんからね。
> (Since I don't have anyone to marry.)

as she always did. Mr. Lerner learned the word *aite* and thought that it meant "someone to marry." Then a few days later, when someone asked Mr. Takada if he wasn't going drinking that evening as he was hurrying home after work, he said

> *Aite-ga inai-kara-ne.*
> (Since I don't have anyone to go with.)

This sentence was exactly the same as the one that Miss Yoshida had used. (*Imasen* is more polite than *inai*.) Mr. Lerner was interested in the way the word *aite* is used, and checked the dictionary; he found a variety of English equivalents such as "companion, partner, pal, mate," and even "rival."

\*　　　\*　　　\*

*Aite* means "someone to do something with." If you marry someone, that person is your *kekkon-no aite* or simply *aite*. If you play *go* with someone, that person is a *go-no aite* or *aite*. If you go drinking with someone, the person is a *sake-no aite* or *aite*. When the situation is provided, such modifiers as *kekkon-no*, *go-no*, or *sake-no* can be left out and simply *aite* used.

Some compounds with *aite* that are often used are: *hanashi-aite* (someone to talk with), *soodan-aite* (someone to turn to for advice), and *asobi-aite* (someone to have fun with).

*Aite* does not always mean someone who is cooperative. If you compete with someone, your rival is a *kyoosoo-aite*. And you need an *aite* to quarrel, too.

If nobody listens to you or cares for you, you may complain, saying

> *Dare-mo aite-ni shite-kurenai.*
> だれも　相手に　してくれない。
> (*lit.* Nobody will treat me as his companion.)

This applies to various situations; it can be that the speaker is disliked because of his personality or actions; it can be that others are too busy. Or, it can be that a country gains too much profit in the international marketplace and all other countries want to stop trading with it.

# Kono-goro doomo chooshi-ga waru-kute. . .

## このごろ どうも 調子が わるくて……

## (Somehow I am in poor condition these days)

During lunch time a few days ago Mr. Kato complained that he was suffering from arthritis. Mr. Lerner felt sorry for him and wanted to ask him to stay home and take good care of himself. Then someone else started complaining about his own arthritis, and another person said that he couldn't sleep well, and another said that he didn't have a good appetite. All of them said

*Kono-goro doomo chooshi-ga warukute . . .*
このごろ どうも 調子が わるくて……
(Somehow I am in poor condition these days.)

When Mr. Kato explained how bad his arthritis was, everyone described his own present or past experience of arthritis. For a while the office looked like a doctor's clinic full of sick people. Mr. Lerner started worrying what would become of the company. But at one o'clock, everyone stopped discussing his sickness and quickly went back to work as if nothing were the matter.

\*      \*      \*

One's sickness seems to be a favorite topic among Japanese, especially among middle-aged people. In offices, stores, or even at home, when several people get together for an idle talk, or before they start a business discussion, they like to talk about sickness they are suffering from. The

14

sickness, however, has to be a mild and non-contagious one; such diseases as typhoid, tuberculosis or cancer cannot be favorite topics. Arthritis, allergies, insomnia, headaches and a sluggish stomach are among the best. Common phrases used in such discussions are:

*Doomo i-no chooshi-ga warukute . . .*
(Somehow my stomach is in poor condition and . . .)
*Doomo shokuyoku-ga nakute . . .*
(Somehow I have a poor appetite and . . .)
*Doomo tsukareyasukute . . .*
どうも　つかれやすくて……
(Somehow I get tired easily and . . .)

The underlying idea behind this love of talking about sicknesses is that it is important to sympathize with others as well as to be sympathized with by others. When someone complains about his poor health, others should express their sympathy, and also complain about themselves. All in all, the Japanese regard it as good to know that everyone is equally suffering from some kind of trouble.

15

# Katta, Katta
## 買った、買った
### (You bought them, you bought them)

Mr. Lerner went to a festival at the shrine in his neighborhood yesterday afternoon. There were several people watching a man selling bananas by the roadside. The spectators looked amused at the way the banana-seller was shouting. So Mr. Lerner joined them and tried to make out what he was saying. The man raised his voice and said

*Saa, katta, katta.*
さあ、買った、買った。
(*lit.* Now you bought them, you bought them.)

Mr. Lerner looked around to see who had bought the bananas, but there was no one who had bananas with him. The salesman repeated the same phrase until one of the spectators stepped up and said

*Yoshi. Katta.* よし。買った。
(*lit.* All right, I bought them.)

Mr. Lerner realized them that the salesman had been using the phrase *katta* to urge the people to buy bananas, but he wondered how the past form of a verb could be used with a future action.

\* \* \*

According to the grammatical explanation Mr. Lerner was given, *ta* is added to verbs to make the past form. (With verbs ending in *gu*,

16

*bu*, *mu*, and *nu*, *da* is added instead of *ta*, *yomu* becomes *yonda* and *shinu* becomes *shinda*.) But it is more correct to say that verbs ending in *ta* or *da* express completion of an action rather than the past tense. This form can be used regardless of the tense; actually it appears both in the past tense and the present. It can even be used in the future; *ashita ichiban hayaku kita hito-ni age-masu* means "I'll give it to the person who will come first tomorrow—*lit.* the person who came first tomorrow." Thus, *megane-o kakeru hito* means "someone who is going to wear glasses" and *megane-o kaketa hito* means "someone who has worn, and is now wearing, glasses."

Verbs ending in *ta* or *da* can also express a command; *katta* can mean "buy it," as the banana salesman said. Similarly one sometimes says *doita, doita* when he wants to say "Get out of the way!"; this is somewhat like the English "Be gone!" meaning "Go away!" in that emphasis is placed on the state which will result from the completion of an action rather than on the action itself.

# *Wakarimashita, hai*
# わかりました、はい
## (Yes, yes, I understand)

Miss Yoshida advised Mr. Lerner to use *ee* to mean "yes" rather than *hai* because *hai* sounded too formal when talking with her. But yesterday afternoon he heard her say on the phone

*Ee, soo-desu, hai.*
(*lit.* Yes, that's right, yes.)

Mr. Lerner felt it strange that she had used both *hai* and *ee* in one sentence. Then she said

**Wakarimashita, hai.**
わかりました、はい。
(*lit.* I understood, yes.)

and hung up rather abruptly. She was apparently irritated by the person on the phone. Mr. Lerner found that *hai* can sound rather rude.

*　　*　　*

To show one's agreement both *hai* and *ee* are used, and in this usage *hai* sounds more formal than *ee*. But *hai* has several other usages besides showing agreement. It is used to mean "I have heard you" or "I understand." As used in Miss Yoshida's answer *Wakarimashita, hai*, *hai* gives an impression of finality. When said bluntly, it can mean "that's enough" or "I don't want to hear any more."

When *hai* is used to show finality, it is said immediately after the preceding phrase or sentence; there is no pause between *Wakarimashita*

18

and *hai*, for example.

Because of this impression of finality, some people add *hai* to their own sentences as in:

*Kinoo itte-kimashita, hai. Demo mitsu-karimasen-deshita, hai. Moo-ichido itte-mimasu, hai.*

(*lit.* I went there yesterday, yes. But I didn't find it, yes. I'll go and see once more, yes.)

Here *hai* is added as if it were a kind of period. Frequent use of *hai* in this way is not recommended because it gives the impression that the speaker is overly anxious to make sure he is understood, or that he is lacking in confidence.

# *Rikutsu*
## りくつ
### (Mere logic)

After a business discussion yesterday afternoon, Mr. Okada started talking about his son
who is now a college student. He complained that
the young man does not listen to him; the explanation he used to describe his son's impertinence
was

> *Rikutsu-bakari itte . . .*
> りくつばかり　言って……
> (*lit.* He talks nothing but logic.)

Since Mr. Lerner didn't know the word *rikutsu* he
consulted a dictionary. He found English equivalents such as "theory," "logic," "argument" and
"pretext." He wondered which of them best suit-
ed the case of Mr. Okada's son.

\*　　　\*　　　\*

The word *rikutsu* itself means "theory" as in
*Rikutsu-to genjitsu-wa chigau* (Things do not actually go as in theory). But very often it is used
in the sense of "mere logic" or "useless argument." When one says *rikutsu-o yuu* (*lit.* to talk
about logic) in a deprecatory tone, he means that
the person argues only to protect his own inter-
ests. Fathers often shout to their sons

> *Rikutsu-o yuu-na.*
> りくつを　言うな。
> (*lit.* Don't talk about logic.)

actually meaning "Don't talk back."

The underlying idea seems to be that it is not desirable to have to discuss theory between family members. Most parents expect that parents and children should understand each other without depending on verbal explanation. They don't like to discuss things with their children as if they were strangers. They are irritated to hear their children's explanations because they feel that the ideal parent-child relations are in jeopardy. Thus, instead of trying to persuade their children, many parents tell them to be quiet.

To some extent this is also seen in social situations. Many bosses feel offended at having to listen to the unnecessary discussion of their workers. They can't say *Rikutsu-o yuu-na* directly to them. So, with their fellow superintendents, they complain that they have to work with youngsters who spend their time

*Rikutsu-bakari itte* . . .
(Talking nothing but logic.)

# Hito
## ひと
### (A person)

Yesterday afternoon at work, Mr. Lerner saw two young women walking down the hall. When he was about to pass by them, one of them asked him if he worked there. He answered in the phrase he thought he had heard others use:

*Ee, watashi-wa koko-no hito-desu-ga . . .*
(*lit.* Yes, I am a person of this place.)

meaning "yes, I work here." The women looked at each other; obviously his Japanese wasn't right. Then Miss Yoshida came and the women turned to her.

Later Miss Yoshida told him that he shouldn't have used the word *hito* (a person). He felt discouraged to know that he wasn't good enough at Japanese to use a simple word like *hito* properly.

&ast;    &ast;    &ast;

Very often basic words are the most difficult to use correctly because they have various usages. *Hito* means "a person" as in *ano hito* (that person), *wakai hito* (young person) and *otoko-no-hito* (man- *lit.* male person). In the biological sense *hito* means "human being" as opposed to animals and other creatures. But in social situations, *hito* refers to someone other than the speaker. Therefore it sounds strange to say *Watashi-wa wakai hito-desu* to mean "I am a young person" or to say *Watashi-wa koko-no hito-desu.*

To refer to oneself, one usually leaves out the

word *hito* or uses *mono*, a humble counterpart of *hito*. Thus, to mean "I work here," one says either

> *Koko-ni tsutomete-imasu.*
> (*lit.* I work here.)
> or
> *Koko-no mono-desu.* ここの 者です。
> (I belong to this place.—*lit.* I am a person of this place.)

When referring to someone else, one says either

> *Koko-no hito-desu.* (He or she works here.)
> or more politely;
> *Koko-no kata-desu.*

You can easily tell that *hito* is used to mean "others" in such sentences as *Hito-wa hito, jibun-wa jibun* (Others are others; oneself is oneself) or *Hito-o tayori-ni shite-wa ikenai* (One shouldn't depend on others).

A special and interesting usage is to refer indirectly to the speaker by *hito* as in

> *Hito-o nan-da-to omotte-iru-n-da.*
> (What do you think I am?—*lit.* What do you think a person is?)
> or
> *Hito-o baka-ni shinaide-kudasai.*
> (Don't make a fool of me.—*lit.* Don't make fools of others.)

# *Muri-o suru*
# むりを する
## (To overdo)

A few weeks ago Mr. Okada complained that he felt very tired. Mr. Takada showed his concern and suggested that he take good care of himself; he added

*Amari muri-o suru-to karada-o kowashimasu-yo.*

あまり 無理を すると 体を こわしますよ。

(If you overwork yourself, you will ruin your health.)

Mr. Lerner liked the expression *muri-o suru* which he was told means "to overwork oneself," because many Japanese seemed to be working too hard. He thought he would use it himself some time.

Then yesterday morning when Mr. Takada came into the office in a new suit, several people said

*Muri-o shimashita-ne.*

Mr. Lerner took it as meaning "You overworked yourself," and wondered why, since Mr. Takada didn't look tired at all.

\*　　　\*　　　\*

According to the dictionary, the word *muri* means "unreasonable," "impossible" or "impracticable." *Muri-o suru* literally means "to do something unreasonable"; it actually means "to do something beyond the reasonable limit" or "to force oneself." Thus, depending on the situation, *muri-o suru* can mean either "to overwork one-self," or "to do something against one's feelings" or even "to spend too much money." By saying *Muri-o shimashita-ne* (You overdid yourself), the colleagues teased Mr. Takada for having spent lavishly on his suit; it could also serve as a compliment by implying that the new suit looked so expensive.

In social situations *muri* is often used in declining someone's request as in

*Chotto muri-kamo shiremasen.*
ちょっと　無理かも　しれません。
(It may be very difficult.—*lit.* it may be a little unreasonable.)

rather than flatly saying *Dekimasen* (I can't do it).

When making a request, too, *muri* is used as in

*Murina onegai-towa omoimasu-ga . . .*
(*lit.* I think it is an unreasonable request, but . . .)

meaning "I know I shouldn't ask you this, but . . ." Or, after making a request, one may add

*Murini-towa mooshimasen-ga.*
(*lit.* I don't say that it should be done unreasonably.)

meaning "I don't mean to inconvenience you by asking too much."

25

## Shujin-ga soo mooshimasu-node
## 主人が　そう　申しますので
### (Since my husband insists on it)

Mr. Lerner was invited by the Takadas to dinner last Sunday. When he was leaving, Mrs. Takada followed him to the door, and asked him to take a box of candies home. Mr. Lerner said that he shouldn't accept it because he had already been treated so generously. Mrs. Takada asked again, and while Mr. Lerner was hesitating, she said

*Shujin-ga soo mooshimasu-node . . .*
主人が　そう　申しますので……
(Since my husband says so . . .)

She implied that if Mr. Lerner didn't take it, she would be embarrassed, so he had to give up and accept the gift. He remembered that Mr. Takada had said that he had drunk too much and couldn't come to the door to say good-bye. He doubted if Mr. Takada was really so drunk.

\*　　　\*　　　\*

People sometimes shift their own responsibility onto someone else. To do so in order to be spared criticism or reprimand is regarded as cowardly by the Japanese, too. But to do this for the purpose of doing favors for others is regarded as good by them. Especially when offering gifts or kindnesses, Japanese often refer to their family members and insist upon acceptance for their sake. The wife will say *Shujin-ga soo mooshimasu* (or, less formally, *iimasu*); in the same manner the husband will say *Kanai-ga . . .* (My

26

wife . . .); and the son or daughter will say *Chichi-ga . . .* (My father . . .) or *Haha-ga. . .* (My mother . . .).

The underlying idea is that it is not desirable to insist on one's own wishes but that it is good to act according to the wishes of someone with whom one identifies oneself. Saying *Shujin-ga* (or *Kanai-ga) soo iimasu-node* also serves to give the impression that the speaker's relations with the spouse are very good.

This reference is also made when making requests or when complaining. For instance, when asking a neighbor to stop playing the piano at night, the speaker may say *Shujin-ga nemu-renai-to yuu mono-desu-kara* (Since my husband says he can't sleep) rather than saying that she herself can't sleep.

# Doo-deshoo-ne
## どうでしょうね
### (I wonder how it is)

When Mr. Lerner and Mr. Takada went to see Mr. Mori, the director, he was reading a plan that someone had made and submitted to him. He showed it to them and when they had read through it, he said

**Kore-wa doo-deshoo-ne.**
これは　どうでしょうね。

Mr. Lerner took this remark to be a question meaning "What do you think about it?" So he started explaining the reasons he didn't think the plan was very good. It was rather difficult to explain and he had to try hard to find the right words. But before he had finished his explanation, Mr. Mori waved his hand as if he didn't want to hear any more, and put the paper away. Mr. Lerner felt offended and turned to Mr. Takada. Mr. Takada told him that the director himself had already expressed a similar opinion about it, and he didn't have to say anything more. Mr. Lerner wondered if he had failed to understand Mr. Mori's words, and felt that he had to practice the aural comprehension of Japanese even harder.

\*　　　\*　　　\*

No, Mr. Lerner didn't make any mistakes in aural comprehension. He had correctly understood the literal meaning of what Mr. Mori had said. But he didn't know that Doo-deshoo-ne said with a doubtful, falling tone usually indicates

28

negative judgment rather than a question. If Mr. Mori had really wanted to hear Mr. Lerner's opinion, he would have said *Doo-deshoo-ne* in a rising tone, or chosen another expression such as

*Kore, doo-deshoo-ka.* or *Kore, doo omoimasu-ka.* これ、どう　思いますか。

meaning "What do you think of this?"

*Doo-deshoo-kane* is used also for negative judgments when said with a doubtful tone.

Saying *Dooka-to omoimasu* expresses negative judgment even more definitely, as in *Ano-hito-no yaru koto-wa dooka-to omoimasu-ne* (He never does things right—*lit.* As for what he does, I think "how is it?"). *Dooka-to omoimasu* is used not only in disapproval but also in apprehension, as in

*Ichiji-wa dooka-to omoimashita-ga.*
(I was apprehensive once.)

This refers either to weather that once seemed threatening and later cleared up or to a very sick person's condition.

# Sonii-san
# ソニーさん
## (Mr. Sony)

Miss Winters told Mr. Lerner the other day that she had been working a few months for a trading company called "Suzuki-Booeki." She said that she had had an interesting experience just a couple of days before.

When she answered the phone, the speaker said

*Moshi-moshi, Suzuki Booeki-san-desu-ka.*

She took it as "Hello, Miss Suzuki-Booeki?" and said "No" instantly, and hung up. But just the next moment she heard one of her colleagues saying

*Sonii-san-desu-ka. Kochira-wa Suzuki-Booeki-desu.* ソニーさんですか。こちらは　鈴木貿易です。

(Hello, Mr. Sony? This is the Suzuki Trading Company.)

\*　　　\*　　　\*

The suffix *san* is added to people's names, both first and last, and to occupations as in *oma-wari-san* (Mr. Policeman). Not only that, it is used with stores, too; *yaoya-san* means either "a greengrocer" or "a vegetable store." Sometimes names of stores are said with *san*, usually by women, as in *Mikawaya-san-de kaimashita* (I bought it at Mikawaya).

In a similar way *san* is added to the name of companies probably because they are person-ified. Most businessmen refer to other companies

30

with *san* as if they were human beings, as in

> *Sonii-san-towa torihiki-ga arimasu.*
> (We deal with Sony.)
> *Hitachi-san-niwa itsumo osewa-ni natte-imasu.*
> 日立さんには いつも お世話に なっております。
> (We deal with Hitachi.—*lit.* Mr. Hitachi is always kind to us.)

It can be said that names of companies are treated like family names; therefore *Sonii-san-wa doo-desu-ka* (How about you, Mr. Sony?) is said to someone from Sony. The idea is that the person belongs to a family whose name is Sony.

But it must be noted that *san* is used in this way only when the speaker is engaged in business with the company or the institution. you can say that *san* is used as an endearment rather than a sign of respect. The teller at the bank will call the owner of the passbook (*tsuuchoo*) to the window saying *Sonii-san* or *Kokuritsu Kokugo Kenkyuujo-san* (Mr. National Language Research Institute), because they are the bank's valued customers.

# *Kikoo-no see-deshoo*
# 気候の　せいでしょう
## (It must be due to the weather)

Mr. Okada always complains about his health before starting business discussions with Mr. Lerner and Mr. Takada. Mr. Lerner is often surprised at the patience Mr. Takada shows when listening to Mr. Okada's complaints. He wouldn't be able to stand so much complaining; he would ask Mr. Okada to go home and stay in bed instead of coming to discuss business. Just yesterday afternoon when Mr. Okada complained about his arthritis as usual, Mr. Takada said quietly,

*Kikoo-no see-deshoo.*
気候の　せいでしょう。
(It must be due to the weather.)

and this seemed to satisfy Mr. Okada. Mr. Lerner decided to say this when he was tempted to say "Go home and stay in bed!"

Mr. Lerner was also interested in the phrase *. . . no see.* He was once told by Sensee to be careful in using it because it has the nuance of a reprimand, so he has not used it yet.

\*　　　\*　　　\*

*See* is used to imply that the speaker is unhappy about the situation or angry with the cause, as in

*Ano-hito-no see-de paatii-ga dame-ni natta.*
(*lit.* Due to him the party became no good.)

which means "he spoiled the party." Therefore

one has to be careful when using *see* with someone's name; the causes which are used very often
in everyday conversation are as follows:

> *sake-no see* 酒の　せい
> (due to alcoholic beverages),
> *toshi-no see* 年の　せい
> (due to age),
> *byooki-no see* 病気の　せい
> (due to sickness), etc.

Nature is so generous that we can place blame
on her easily.

> *Atsusa-no see-de shigoto-ga hakadorimasen.*
> (Due to the heat, we aren't making much
> progress on the work.)

When one is happy about the situation, *okage*
is used to indicate the reason as in

> *Ano-hito-no okage-de umaku itta.*
> (Thanks to him, it went well.)
> *Renshuu-shita okage-de yoku dekita.*
> (Because I practiced hard, I could do it
> well.)

Our students often use *tame* to indicate the
cause as in

> *Atsusa-no tame-ni shigoto-ga hakadorima-
> sen.*

This is correct but not quite conversational. *Tame*
is used mostly to mean "for the sake of" or "for
the benefit of" rather than "due to." To show the
cause, either *see* or *okage* is preferred in conversation because it reflects the speaker's emotions.

# *Ookuri-shimashoo*
## お送りしましょう
### (I'll see you off)

Mr. Lerner went to Mr. Okada's office to discuss some business a few days ago. When he had finished the discussion and was going to leave, Mr. Okada said

*Ookuri-shimashoo.*
お送りしましょう。
(I'll go with you.)

and opened the door as usual. While walking toward the subway station with Mr. Okada, Mr. Lerner wondered if the expression *ookuri-shimashoo* comes from the verb *okuru* that is used for sending things. It was not like Mr. Okada, who is always very polite, to treat others like a parcel. When he returned to the office and asked Miss Yoshida about it, she said she had never thought about it before.

\*　　　\*　　　\*

*Ookuri-shimashoo* (*lit.* I'll send you) is a humble form derived from the verb *okuru*. When this verb is used with a person, it means "to escort someone" either in a vehicle or by walking together. "To escort" may sound like a man going with a woman, but *okuru* refers to a woman going with a man, too, so it is more correct to say "to see someone either to his destination or part of the way there."

The Japanese regard it as more polite to go with the visitor all the way to his home; in this case one says

34

*Otaku-made ookuri-shimashoo.*
(I'll see you home.)

But actually one often sees the visitor only part of the way; then one says

*Sono hen-made ookuri-shimashoo.*
その　へんまで　お送りしましょう。
(I'll walk with you a little way down the street.)

When one is busy working and cannot go with the visitor, one apologizes by saying

*Ookuri-mo shimasen-de.*
(I'm sorry I can't see you home.)

Or, one says *Koko-de shitsuree-shimasu* (Please excuse me here) when parting at the door.

Nowadays many Japanese are too busy to see their visitors home, or even to the subway station, but they still feel that they should; they are sorry that they cannot stick to the old custom of spending much time on meeting and seeing off visitors.

# *Sore-wa sore-wa*
## それは　それは
### (Oh, that is. . . .)

Mr. Lerner dropped in at Professor Taka-hashi's house the other day. Professor Takahashi had asked him to check his translation. He had said that he would come to Mr. Lerner's office to get it when it was finished. But Mr. Lerner had some business in the neighborhood, so he thought he would take it to Professor Takahashi. When he explained why he had come unexpectedly, Professor Takahashi said

> *Sore-wa sore-wa.*
> それは　それは。
> (*lit*. That is, that is.)

and asked him to come in. Mr. Lerner guessed that this phrase must be an expression of thanks, and answered *iie*.

A few days later, however, he found that it is used not only for expressing gratitude. When he told another acquaintance about his working for a Japanese company, she said *Sore-wa sore-wa*.

\*　　　\*　　　\*

*Sore-wa sore-wa* can be taken as the first part of a sentence such as *Sore-wa arigatoo-go-zaimasu* (That's very kind of you) or *Sore-wa kek-koo-desu-ne* (That's very nice); *sore-wa* is re-peated for emphasis.

It is used as a polite expression of thanks for a favor. It indicates that the speaker is surprised at the unusually big favor. In response to some-one else's statement, it is used to express one's surprise accompanied by admiration. This expression is polite and formal, and used more often by older people than by young people.

The phrase is composed of two *sore-wa*s which should be pronounced in succession with no pause after the first *sore-wa*. And it sounds more polite when said slowly.

Mr. Lerner was right when he answered *lie* to Professor Takahashi's *Sore-wa sore-wa*. To someone's admiration, too, one usually says *lie* shortly and goes on to the next statement. In short, when someone has said *Sore-wa sore-wa* to him, the listener should politely accept it and does not have to say much in response.

## *Okutte-kimashita*
## 送ってきました
## (He sent it to me)

Mr. Lerner received a book from Mr. Kawakami yesterday. He wanted to tell Miss Yoshida about it in the office this morning. He said

*Kawakami-san-ga hon-o okurimashita.*

meaning "Mr. Kawakami sent me a book." He purposely left out *watashi-ni* (to me) because adding it would sound like a direct translation from English. But Miss Yoshida asked *Dare-ni* (To whom?). Then, should Mr. Lerner have said *Kawakami-san-ga watashi-ni hon-o okurimashita?*

\*     \*     \*

Mr. Lerner should have said

**Kawakami-san-ga hon-o okutte-kimashita.**
川上さんが　本を　送ってきました。

Saying *Kawakami-san-ga hon-o okurimashita* sounds incomplete because it does not say to whom Mr. Kawakami sent the book. It is not natural to say *Kawakami-san-ga watashi-no hon-o okurimashita* either, because it sounds like a description of an action which has nothing to do with the speaker. In Japanese what directly concerns the speaker has to be expressed in a way different from describing what has happened to others. The English "to me" or "me" is very often expressed in phrases other than *watashi-ni* or *watashi-o*.

One of those phrases is to add *kuru* to the *-te*

form of the verb; *kuru* indicates that someone's action affects the speaker. When something has been sent to the speaker, he says *okutte-kimashita* (he sent it to me) instead of saying *watashi-ni okurimashita*. When referring to what has been said in someone's letter, the speaker says *Kawakami-san-ga ii-to itte-kimashita* (Mr. Kawakami wrote to me that it is all right).

In a similar way, instead of saying *Kawakami-san-ga watashi-ni denwa-o kakemashita*, one usually says *Kawakami-san-ga denwa-o kakete-kimashita* to mean "Mr. Kawakami called me."

The following expressions with *kuru* are used very often in daily conversation.

> *todokete-kimashita* (he delivered it to me)
> *hakonde-kimashita* (he brought it to me)
> *shirasete-kimashita* (he informed me of it)
> *renraku-shite-kimashita* (he contacted me)

# *Otaku*
## お宅
### (You)

The other day several people came from another company to discuss business with Mr. Takada and Mr. Lerner. After the discussions they went to a restaurant and had lunch together. When they were talking about golf, one of them turned to Mr. Takada and asked

> *Otaku-wa doo-desu-ka.*
> お宅は　どうですか。
> (*lit.* How about your house?)

Mr. Lerner thought that the question was about whether or not Mr. Takada's family liked golf, but Mr. Takada said that he didn't play it much and said *Kochira-wa joozu-desu-ga* (He's good, though—*lit.* This side is good but), indicating Mr. Lerner.

\*　　　\*　　　\*

*Otaku* literally means "honorable house" and is used in such phrases as *Mori-san-no otaku* (Mr. Mori's house) or *minasan-no otaku* (your houses). When it is used by itself, it means either "your house" or "someone's house" with respect, as in *Otaku-no minasan ogenki-desu-ka* (Is everyone at your house fine?). Or it refers to family members as in *Otaku-wa minasan uta-ga ojoozu-desu-ne* (All your family members are good singers).

Between employees of different companies, *otaku* is often used to refer to the company to which the listener belongs, as in *Otaku-wa keeki-*

*ga ii-deshoo* (Your company must be enjoying good business).

Sometimes this word is used to mean "you." *Anata* (you) is rather limited in usage, and various other terms are used to address the listener. Most often the listener's name is used as in *Yamada-san-wa doo omoimasu-ka* ( *lit*. What does Mr. Yamada think about it?), meaning "What do you think about it?" Sometimes terms indicating the listener's position such as *sensee* (teacher) or *okusan* (wife) are used.

When *otaku* is used to mean "you," it does not imply respect, and sounds rather impersonal. Because of this, it has come to be used frequently by people working for the mass media. In this field, people often have to converse with someone whose name or status is not known, and *otaku* seems to work well in such cases.

*Otaku* is not used with someone one knows well or respects. If it is used between good friends, the speaker is teasing the listener by acting as if they were strangers.

# Kaerasete-itadakimasu
## 帰らせていただきます
### (I'm going home)

Mr. Lerner sometimes watches family dramas on TV, a type of program he seldom watched before coming to Japan, because they seem to offer a good chance to observe how Japanese is used in daily life. Just a few days ago, in one of these dramas, he saw a man and his wife having a serious quarrel. The angry wife said

*Watashi, uchi-e kaerasete-itadakimasu.*
わたし、うちへ　帰らせていただきます。
(*lit.* I will receive your kindness of letting me go home.)

meaning that she was going to leave her husband and go back to her parents' home. He asked Miss Yoshida about this expression the next day and learned that it is more polite than saying *Watashi, uchi-e kaerimasu* just as saying *yasumasete-itadakimasu* is more polite than *yasumimasu* (I'll be absent from work). He wondered if Japanese wives use polite terms even when they quarrel with their husbands.

\*　　　\*　　　\*

Making the tone of speech more polite shows that the relationship between the speaker and the listener has become a distant one. In quarrels, some people call their opponents insulting names like *baka* (fool), *manuke* (stupid) and others, but some people make their tone of speech politer than usual. The difference is that insults are used by unsophisticated people, or when the speaker does not want to behave in a sophisticated manner, whereas polite expressions are used when the speaker wants to be sophisticated or reserved. Women use the second method more often than men because they want to look sophisticated or because they have been trained to do so.

Polite terms are sometimes also used to show criticism or sarcasm. A mother will change the term *Makoto-chan* to *Makoto-san*, which sounds more formal, when she is going to scold her son. This is similar to the English-speaking mother calling her son "Richard" or "Richard Stevens" instead of "Dick" when she scolds him.

What matters is the change from the usual tone. If your listener has suddenly changed his tone and made it even politer than usual when not making a difficult request or apology, it is very likely that he is angry with you.

# Senpai

# 先輩

## (Senior)

Yesterday afternoon a man came to see Mr. Takada at the office. Mr. Takada introduced him, Mr. Hotta, to Mr. Lerner and the other people working with him. He told them that Mr. Hotta had been one year senior to him at college. It was almost time to leave the office, and Mr. Takada asked him in a very polite tone if he would go somewhere together with him. Then Mr. Hotta answered in quite a casual way

*Un, meshi-demo kuoo-ka.*
(Yeah, let's eat.)

Even the director of the company wouldn't talk to Mr. Takada in such a rough way, so Mr. Lerner was surprised. Before leaving the office, Mr. Hotta turned to the people there and said with a bow

*Koitsu-o dooka yoroshiku onegai-shimasu.*
(Please be good to him.—*lit.* I ask you to take good care of this fellow.)

as if he were Mr. Takada's father or older brother.

\*        \*        \*

The relationship between a *senpai* (senior person) and a *koohai* (junior person) is very distinct among Japanese students. Especially among students who belong to the same group in sports or other activities, a *senpai* is regarded as

44

absolutely superior and a *koohai* has to obey him unconditionally. On the other hand, a *senpai* is supposed to teach his *koohai* kindly and be as protective as a father. This is not limited to men students; women have similar relations, especially among those who belong to the same sports team.

In speech, too, a *senpai* talks like a boss and a *koohai* like a subordinate. This distinction is observed even more strictly than between a teacher and a student. These days teachers are often rather polite and sometimes yielding to their students, but a *senpai* is as strict as an officer with a private in the army.

And this relationship usually remains the same even after both the *senpai* and the *koohai* have graduated from school. Thus Mr. Hotta behaved as a *senpai* to Mr. Takada at the office, although Mr. Takada is now a working man and a master of a household. Sometimes both the *senpai* and the *koohai* work for the same company; the situation is quite awkward when the *koohai* happens to be promoted faster and placed above his *senpai*.

## *Korekara doko-e iku-no*
## これから　どこへ　行くの
### (Where are you going now?)

When Mr. Lerner was walking with Mr. Takada the other day, they happened to meet Mrs.
Kato, the wife of one of their colleagues. She was
with her little boy about 5 or 6 years old. After
the two men had greeted her rather politely, Mr.
Takada turned to the boy and asked

> *Korekara doko-e iku-no.*
> これから　どこへ　行くの。
> (Where are you going now?)

in a gentle tone. The boy answered happily

> *Doobutsuen-e iku-no.*
> 動物園へ　行くの。
> (We're going to the zoo.)

This was a very simple conversation, but Mr.
Lerner was interested in the use of *no* in their
sentences. He had been told that mostly women
use *no* at the end of a sentence, but both Mr. Takada and the boy had used it.

\*　　　\*　　　\*

The particle *no* is added either to a question
or a statement; when the sentence is said with a
rising tone, it is a question, and when said with a
falling tone, it is a statement. So Mr. Takada
said *Korekara doko-e iku-no* with a rising tone,
and the boy answered *Doobutsuen-e iku-no* with
a falling tone.

Sentences ending in *no* are considered to be

46

feminine or childish. When *no* is added to the plain form, it sounds familiar; such sentences are used mostly by women or children. When *no* is added to a polite sentence, it sounds exclusively feminine; *Doobutsuen-e ikimasu-no* is said only by women.

Mr. Takada used a sentence ending in the plain form plus *no* because he was talking to a little boy. There is a tendency for the speaker to change his tone according to the listener. (cf.*Nihongo Notes 1*, pp. 128-129).

Other particles can be added to *no*; *Doobutsu-en-e iku-no-ne* (You're going to the zoo, aren't you?) and *Doobutsuen-e iku-no-yo* (We ARE going to the zoo) are said mostly by children, or women in familiar speech. Women will say *Ashi-ta-wa oyasumi-desu-no-ne* (The store is closed tomorrow, isn't it?) and *Ee, soo-na-n-desu-no-yo* (Yes, that's right).

## *Doo-itashimashite*
## どういたしまして
## (You're welcome)

These days Mr. Lerner finds it rather diffi-cult to respond appropriately to the polite expres-sions of thanks said by people working in stores or restaurants. When he was first learning Japa-nese, a salesman said *Maido arigatoo-gozaimasu* (Thank you very much for your patronage) to him, and he responded

*Doo-itashimashite.*  どういたしまして。
(You're welcome),

but the man looked surprised. After that he stopped using it and tried to observe how the Japanese responded. He found that most of the customers said nothing to this expression of thanks, so he did that for a while. But he didn't like the idea of remaining silent when thanked by someone very politely. Then Mr. Takada told him that he can say *Doomo* (Thanks) in such cases.

\*         \*         \*

*Doo-itashimashite* is a polite denial of what has been said. When it is said to "Thank you," it means "Not at all." When said to a compliment like *Nihongo-ga ojoozu-desu-ne* (You speak Japa-nese very well), it means "Far from it." This ex-pression is rather formal and sounds too weighty for casual occasions. In informal speech, *Iie* (No) is used in its place.

But a customer usually does not use either *Doo-itashimashite* or *Iie* to a storekeeper. Japa-nese seem to use a particular pattern of exchange when they are placed in a customer-salesman relationship.

A customer leaving a store usually says nothing to the storekeeper's *Maido arigatoo-gozaimasu*. Or, when a customer enters a store and is greeted with *Irasshaimase* いらっしゃいませ。 (I'm glad you came), he usually says nothing or just nods in reply. Some customers may say *Doomo* and some *Gochisoosama* (Thanks for the feast) in restaurants; some will say *Osewasama* (Thanks for your trouble) when they feel they have caused extra trouble. But these replies are not required; a customer can remain silent without being regarded as impolite.

This is because the customer and the salesman are conversing according to what might be called a "professional" pattern rather than a "personal" one. If the customer and the storekeeper happen to be acquaintances, they converse according to the "personal" pattern.

## *Okusan-ga osan-demo*
## 奥さんが　お産でも
### (Even if his wife was delivering a baby)

Mr. Lerner was reading about Tokyo in the Edo Period and learned that there were many fires which spread quickly because the houses were made of wood. He also read that many people would run to watch a fire as a kind of amusement; some were so fond of fires that they would leave anything or anybody behind to run to watch them.

To describe this to the people at the office, Mr. Lerner said,

*Okusan-wa osan-demo.*

meaning ''even if his wife was delivering a baby.'' But Miss Yoshida and the other listeners looked strange for a moment and then corrected his words to

*Okusan-**ga** osan-demo.*
奥さんが　お産でも。

How particular Japanese are about particles, Mr. Lerner felt. Do they really distinguish the particles *ga* and *wa* so precisely? They seem to skip particles just as they like, so why do they want foreigners to observe grammar so strictly?

\*　　\*　　\*

The distinction between *ga* and *wa* bothers foreigners who want to speak Japanese correctly, and even teachers of Japanese sometimes find it difficult to explain. There are several differences, but the difference observed in Mr. Lerner's sentence is a basic one. Namely, while *wa* is used to indicate the subject matter, *ga* is used in giving a condition as in *Tenki-ga yokereba ikimasu* (I will go if the weather is good).

Therefore if Mr. Lerner had said *Okusan-ga osan-demo*, it would mean "even if his wife was delivering a baby," the husband would go to see a fire. But since he said *Okusan-wa osan-demo*, it sounded as if the man's wife herself would run to watch a fire while delivering a baby—something quite unrealistic and funny.

In the same way, if someone says

*Watashi-ga yametara* . . .
わたしが　やめたら……
(If I should quit the job . . . )

the rest concerns someone else, so it is usually followed by such conclusions as "you will be inconvenienced." If someone says

*Watashi-wa yametara*. . .
わたしは　やめたら……

what follows concerns the speaker himself, so the listener will expect him to say something like "I want to move to the seaside."

# *Kusuri-o nondemo*
## くすりを のんでも
### (Even if I take medicine)

Mr. Lerner has been unable to sleep well these days, and he had a headache yesterday afternoon. So he said he would leave early. Miss Yoshida looked concerned and brought him some pills. But Mr. Lerner knew that he needed rest, not medicine, so he said

*Kusuri-o nomeba naorimasen.*

meaning "Taking medicine will not cure it." Miss Yoshida laughed and said that she didn't have to worry about his headache because he was able to make such a clever joke.

He did not understand at the time, but after resting awhile at home, he realized that he should have said

*Kusuri-o **nondemo** naorimasen.*
くすりを のんでも なおりません。
\*　　　\*　　　\*

Verbs ending in the *-eba* form like *nomeba* (and adjectives ending in *-kereba* like *yasukereba*) are used to indicate a condition which leads to an expected result. For instance, usually people like to buy things at low prices, so it is natural to say

*Yasuku nareba kaimasu.*
(I'll buy it if it becomes cheaper.)
　or
*Yasukereba kaimasu.*
(I'll buy it if it is cheap.)

52

In the same way, people usually expect that taking medicine will cure a sickness, so saying

*Kusuri-o nomeba naorimasu.*
(If you take medicine, you'll be cured.)

sounds natural.

On the other hand, verbs ending in *-temo* or *-demo* are used when the result is not what the speaker or the listener expects or wishes. So, Mr. Lerner should have said

*Kusuri-o nondemo naorimasen.*

because he knew that he had to have a rest rather than medicine. But saying *Kusuri-o nomeba naorimasen* meant "If I take medicine, I'm sure I won't be cured." and it was taken as a sarcasm about the ineffectiveness of medicine.

When phrases indicating conditions thus foretell what follows, the speaker does not have to complete his sentences. For instance, when people are discussing if they can be in time for a train, saying

*Isogeba . . .*　　いそげば……
(If you hurry . . .)

is enough to mean that they'll be able to make it, and

*Isoidemo . . .*　　いそいでも……

means that they can't make it even if they hurry. Leaving out such phrases as *ma-ni aimasu* (you'll be in time) or *ma-ni aimasen* (you won't be in time) in such cases is quite natural.

53

# *Minna-no okashi*
# みんなの　おかし
## (Everyone's cake)

During the coffee break the other day Miss Yoshida served Mr. Lerner and the others pieces of cake. She went away to help someone without sitting down to eat. When she returned and asked Mr. Lerner if he wanted some more cake, he said that he didn't want any more, and added

*Minna-no okashi-o tabemashita-kara.*

meaning "I ate all my cake." After saying it, he felt that his expression was not right, and corrected himself by saying

*Okashi-o **minna** tabemashita-kara.*

Then Miss Yoshida looked relieved. He wondered what difference there was between saying *minna-no okashi* and *okashi-o minna*; he felt the latter was better somehow but didn't know why Miss Yoshida had looked a little puzzled at *minna-no okashi*.

\*　　　\*　　　\*

Words indicating number or quantity are used either before the nouns they modify or after them. You can say either

*Mittsu-no ringo-o kaimashita.*
三つの　りんごを　買いました。
　or
*Ringo-o mittsu kaimashita.*
りんごを　三つ　買いました。

54

to mean "I bought three apples." Both expressions are grammatically correct, but the latter is more appropriate.

This applies to such words as *minna* (all), *sukoshi* (a little) and *hanbun* (half). But the word *minna* can mean "everyone" or "all of us," too; *minna-no okashi* can mean "cake belonging to all of us." Therefore Miss Yoshida was puzzled and worried when he said *Minna-no okashi-o tabemashita*, which could mean "I ate the cakes for all of us." In the same way, saying

*Minna-no okane-o tsukaimashita.*

can mean that you have embezzled some public money instead of meaning that you have spent all of your own money.

Saying *mittsu-no ringo* implies that you are referring to specific apples, so *mittsu-no ringo* corresponds to the English "the three apples" rather than "three apples." Therefore it is quite natural to say

*Mittsu-no ringo-wa oishikatta-desu.*

to mean "The three apples were delicious." But when you want to say you bought three apples, it is more appropriate to say *Ringo-o mittsu kaimashita.*

## *Asobi-ni kita wake-ja arimasen*
## あそびに　来た　わけじゃ　ありません
### (I didn't come for fun)

Yesterday afternoon when Mr. Lerner was having tea with his colleagues, one of them asked him what famous places he had visited in Japan. When they found out that he had not visited many places, they wondered why. Mr. Lerner explained that he had been busy working and studying Japanese, and added

*Nihon-e asobi-ni kimasen-deshita.*

to mean "I didn't come to Japan to have a good time." The listeners didn't understand for a moment, and Miss Yoshida quickly gave a better version, as usual, by way of asking him a question. She said

**Asobi-ni kita wake-ja arimasen-ne.**
あそびに　来た　わけじゃ　ありませんね。
(You didn't come here for fun, did you?)

Mr. Lerner agreed, and remembered that his teacher had told him that he should be careful about partial negation in Japanese.

\*　　　\*　　　\*

Saying *asobi-ni kimasen-deshita* can mean that the speaker didn't come at all. In the same way, saying *minna wakarimasen-deshita* can mean that the speaker didn't understand at all rather than that he didn't understand all. To indicate that part of the sentence is in the negative, *wake-ja arimasen* is used as well as several other devices.

Saying *asobi-ni kita wake-ja arimasen* means that the speaker admits that he came, but that his purpose was not *asobi* (fun). In this usage, the word *wake* means "situation" rather than "reason"; the literal translation would be "The situation isn't that I came for fun."

This can be used to negate words indicating number or quantity as in

*Minna wakatta wake-ja arimasen.*
(I didn't understand all.)
*Zenbu owatta wake-ja arimasen.*
ぜんぶ おわった わけじゃ ありません。
(I haven't finished it all.)

*Wake-ja arimasen* can be used to negate words indicating manner or reason, too. Suppose a husband, a business man, comes home late at night, after drinking with his co-workers. He may say to his wife who criticizes him

*Nomitakute nonde-iru wake-ja nai.*
(I don't drink because I want to.)

This implies that he has to drink for social reasons, not because he likes to drink.

# 'Hai'-to 'lie'
# 「はい」と「いいえ」
## ('Yes' and 'No')

During the tea time yesterday afternoon Miss Yoshida placed a bowl of chocolates on the table and left the room for the tea pot. When she returned and looked at the bowl, she seemed to be wondering about something. Then she turned to Mr. Takada and said half-jokingly

*Takada-san, kore, tabemasen-deshita-ka.*
(Didn't you eat some of this, Mr. Takada?)

Mr. Takada looked surprised and answered quickly

*lie, tabemasen-deshita-yo.*
いいえ、たべませんでしたよ。
(No, I didn't eat any.)

Mr. Lerner thought that *Ee* should have been used in place of *lie*. He had learned that Japanese answer negative questions differently from English-speaking people. Namely, while English-speaking people say ''No'' when agreeing to a negative question as in

A: Didn't you go with him?
B: No, I didn't.

Japanese say *Ee* or *Hai* (more polite) as in

A: *Issho-ni ikimasen-deshita-ka.*
B: *Ee* (or *Hai*), *ikimasen-deshita.* (*lit.* Yes, I

58

didn't go.)

Therefore Mr. Takada should have said

> *Ee, tabemasen-deshita.*
> ええ、たべませんでした。

because he was agreeing with Miss Yoshida's question.

\*　　　\*　　　\*

It is true that the listener answers *Hai* or *Ee* if he agrees with the speaker regardless of whether what follows is in the negative or affirmative. But the most important question is what is meant by "agree." In social communication the listener answers *Hai* when he is going to comply with the speaker's expectation or intent, rather than with a fact the speaker has referred to. Therefore it is possible that either *Hai (Ee)* or *Iie* can be used to answer the same question, depending on the situation.

If Miss Yoshida had asked *Kore, tabemasen-deshita-ka* simply to make sure that Mr. Takada hadn't eaten some of the chocolates, he would have answered *Ee* to show his agreement. But actually she sounded as if she suspected that Mr. Takada had eaten the chocolates before he was asked to, and the question implied criticism. Consequently Mr. Takada said *Iie* to show his denial of her suspicion.

There are exceptions to this use of *hai* and *iie* and some, mostly young, people use *hai* and *iie* more like English-speaking people. But fundamentally the use of "yes" and "no" in Japanese is determined by the relationship between the speaker and the listener, rather than by sheer facts.

# Omachidoosama
## お待ちどおさま
### (Sorry I kept you waiting)

Yesterday Mr. Takada called a sushi shop near the office at noon and asked them to bring some sushi for lunch. The delivery took some time. Mr. Takada had to wait a long time before the young man came in with the sushi. The young man started saying, as usual

*Omachidoosama—*
お待ちどおさま。
(I'm sorry I kept you waiting.)

But when he saw that Mr. Takada looked rather angry he immediately corrected himself and said

*Omatase-shimashita.*
お待たせしました。

which seemed to Mr. Lerner to mean exactly the same thing. He wondered what difference there was between the two expressions.

\* \* \*

As far as the literal meaning goes, the two expressions seem to have similar meanings; *Omachidoosama* literally means "You have been kept waiting for a long time," and *Omatase-shimashita*, "I kept you waiting." But there are some differences in their usage.

One difference is that *Omachidoosama* is used mainly by people engaged in serving customers. A delivery man usually says *Omachidoosama* when he gives the customer what he has been

60

asked to bring. But it is used only when the customer has not been kept waiting for a long time. When he has, *Omachidoosama* is replaced by *Omatase-shimashita*. It seems that *Omachidoosama* has lost most of its original meaning and is used to mean only something like "Here you are." Thus, when compared with *Omatase-shimashita*, *Omachidoosama* sounds more casual and less polite.

Needless to say, it depends on the individual whether he feels that he has kept his customer waiting for a long time or not. So some people may choose *Omatase-shimashita* when others choose *Omachidoosama*. But generally speaking, "quality" restaurants seem to use *Omatase-shimashita* more often.

In personal, rather than professional, situations, *Omachidoosama* is used only to younger people or when one doesn't have to be polite. A parent may say *Omachidoosama* to his child when he has kept him waiting for a little while. Still, this is not appropriate when he has kept him waiting for a long time. Teachers of Japanese often feel embarrassed when their students say *Omachidoosama* to them without meaning to be impolite.

# Kore, agemasu

## これ、あげます

### (I'll give this to you)

When Mr. Lerner went to Kyoto last week, he bought a package of green tea. He wanted to give it to Mr. Mori, the director of the company, who likes good tea. While handing the package to Mr. Mori, he said

   *Kore, tsumaranai mono-desu-ga, agemasu.*
   (This is very little.—*lit.* This is a trifling thing—but I'll give it to you.)

Mr. Mori thanked him, but Mr. Lerner felt something was wrong with his Japanese, so he corrected himself and said

   *Kore, sashiagemasu.* (I'll give this to you.)

because he had learned that *sashiageru* is more humble than *ageru*. But from Mr. Mori's look, this expression did not seem quite appropriate either.

\* \* \*

Dictionaries give several words corresponding to the English "give" such as *yaru*, *ageru*, and *sashiageru*. Grammar books explain that *sashiageru* is the most polite of those three and should be used when giving something to your superior. But when one actually gives something in a social situation, *sashiageru* is not necessarily the most appropriate expression.

It is not quite appropriate to use any word directly meaning "to give" in social situations, just

62

as *kau* (to buy) is not usually used when buying things. A customer says *Sore, kudasai* (Please give it to me) or *Sore, moraimashoo* (I'll take it) rather than saying *Sore, kaimasu* (I'll buy it).

To be polite when giving a present, one chooses from different expressions such as:

> *Yoroshikattara meshiagatte-kudasai.*
> よろしかったら　めしあがってください。
> (Please eat it if it's all right.)
> *Yoroshikattara otsukai-kudasai.*
> (Please use it if it's all right.)
> *Doozo oosame-kudasai.*
> (Please accept it.)

Or, one chooses to sound apologetic as in

> *Tsumaranai mono-desu-ga . . .*
> つまらない　ものですが……
> (This is very little, but . . .)
> *Honno hitokuchi-desu-ga . . .*
> ほんの　一口ですが……
> (This is very little.—*lit.* It's just one mouthful—but . . .)

After these apologetic remarks, such expressions as *Doozo* (Please) or *Doozo meshiagatte-kusasai* are often left out. And even when they are said, they're pronounced rather softly.

# Watashi makemashita-wa
## わたし　まけましたわ
### (I was defeated)

At lunch time the other day Miss Yoshida asked Mr. Lerner what he thought the opposite of

*Watashi makemashita-wa*

was. Since that means "I was defeated," Mr. Lerner answered that it should be *Watashi kachimashita-wa* (I won). But Miss Yoshida said that he was wrong and that the correct answer could be obtained by saying the sentence backwards. So Mr. Lerner started writing it in Roman letters; it went *aw atihsamek. . .* and it didn't make any sense. Mr. Lerner gave up. Miss Yoshida gleefully said it was *Watashi makemashita-wa*, and wrote it down in *hiragana*: わたしまけましたわ

\*　　　\*　　　\*

When Japanese think of the Japanese sounds constituting words, they think of them in the *hiragana* transcription. According to their thinking, *watashi* is not composed of three vowels and three consonants; it is composed of three sounds, *wa*, *ta*, and *shi*. (わ、た、し)

Thus quite a few words can be said backwards and still make sense:

*ta-ka* (eagle) — *ka-ta* (shoulder)
たか——かた
*ba-ka* (fool) — *ka-ba* (hippopotamus)
ばか——かば

64

Not only words, but also some phrases can be said backwards, as in

Watashi makemashita-wa. There are some others like:

Na-tsu-ma-de ma-tsu-na.
なつまでまつな
(Don't wait till summer.)
Ka-n-ke-i na-i ke-n-ka.
かんけいないけんか
(A quarrel that has nothing to do with me)

There is a play on words that many children like; they ask someone what the opposite of tebu-kuro (glove) is, and when they hear the answer ro-ku-bu-te, they instantly hit the person six times, because this literally means "hit six." Sometimes Japanese use kanji to make words that can be read either from the right or the left, or from the top or the bottom (according to the traditional way of writing) as in Yama-moto-yama. 山本山

Mr. Lerner couldn't answer Miss Yoshida's question, but if he wants to return tit for tat, he should ask her what she thinks the opposite of Akasaka is. She would write it in hiragana, and wouldn't easily think of the right answer, which can be obtained by writing it in Roman letters as A-k-a-s-a-k-a.

## 'Ha ha ha'-to 'ho ho ho'
## 「ハハハ」と「ホホホ」
### ('Ha ha ha' and 'ho ho ho')

During the coffee break the other day Mr. Lerner heard Miss Yoshida laughing happily over something. He liked the way she laughed so he said while approaching her

*Mata wa ha ha ha-tte waratte-imasu-ne.*

meaning "you're laughing so happily again." He meant it to be a compliment, but Miss Yoshida didn't like it. When he asked her what he should have said, she answered

*Watashi, ho ho ho-tte waratte-ru-deshoo?*
（Don't you think I'm laughing ho ho ho?）

Mr. Lerner couldn't agree immediately; he felt that *ho ho ho* sounded like Santa Claus laughing. Then the others who were there laughed and said that *ho ho ho* is overly feminine and didn't suit her. Finally they decided that her laughter should be described as *ha ha ha*, although she was not quite satisfied.

\*　　　\*　　　\*

*Ho ho ho* or *o ho ho* is used in Japanese to describe suppressed feminine laughter. When a novelist describes a woman laughing *ho ho ho*, the reader imagines a refined, elegant woman laughing softly, looking down or hiding her mouth with her hand. Many Japanese feel that it is not modest to show the inside of the mouth in public; in this sense *ho ho ho* is appropriate because one

66

does not open the mouth too much when pronouncing the *o* sound. On the other hand the *a* sound requires opening the mouth widely, so *ha ha ha* or *a ha ha* is used to describe an open, frank, wholehearted laughter. Miss Yoshida herself would like to have her laughter described with *ho ho ho*, but her colleagues thought that she was more open and lively than that.

Probably her laughter actually sounded like *wa ha ha ha*, as Mr. Lerner described it. But in the Japanese notion, *wa ha ha ha* is used for someone very masculine and stout, big hearted but coarse, laughing away someone's timid fears. Thus it is quite inappropriate for a young woman. Onomatopoeic words are not always realistic descriptions of actual sounds; Japanese laugh according to the Japanese description, just as English dogs bowwow or yelp while Japanese dogs are supposed to go *wan wan* or *kyan kyan*.

# *Koo yuu mono-desu*
# こう いう 者です
## (My name is this)

A few weeks ago Mr. Lerner received a visitor in his office. The man, a Mr. Kawakami, handed him his name card, saying

*Koo yuu mono-desu-ga.*
こう いう 者ですが。

which literally means "I am the person who is called this way, but." Mr. Lerner had probably heard this expression several times before, but this person said it very clearly so that he could make out the whole sentence.

After that Mr. Lerner began paying attention to what Japanese say when introducing themselves. Many Japanese do not say anything when they offer their name cards, and some use this expression *Koo yuu mono-desu* instead of saying *Kawakami-desu* (I am Mr. Kawakami). This seems quite strange to Mr. Lerner because the *kanji* readings used for Japanese names are often very hard to figure out.

\* \* \*

Many Japanese hand over their name cards without pronouncing their names. Sometimes a person meets another through someone else's introduction either by writing or by telephoning beforehand. In such cases, it is possible to say

*Yamashita-san-kara goshookai-itadaita Kawakami-desu.*
(I'm Kawakami. Mr. Yamashita introduced

me to you.)

But actually many people say

Yamashita-san-kara    goshookai-itadaita    mono-desu.
山下さんから　ご紹介いただいた　者です。
(I am the person Mr. Yamashita introduced to you.)

ignoring his own name, as if the introducer's name is more important than his own.

There seem to be several reasons for this custom. Some people say that Japanese think more of the visual sense than the aural; they usually like to see things rather than to hear things. Another reason is that in many cases Japanese know each other's names before actually meeting, so they do not have to pronounce their names, and this custom has been carried over into cases where two people meet for the first time without knowing each other's names as well. And some people say that Japanese are not as interested in the individual as in the group to which the person belongs.

# *Uso*
## うそ
### (A lie)

Miss Yoshida introduced Mr. Lerner to her sister Michiko the other day. When she said that Mr. Lerner speaks good Japanese and never speaks English with her, Michiko said instantly

*Uso.* うそ。(A lie.)

Mr. Lerner was surprised at her impoliteness and turned to her sister, but Miss Yoshida did not seem embarrassed at all.

After talking a while with Michiko, Mr. Lerner found that she was a sweet, innocent girl. He did not understand why she had spoken so rudely at first. But when he was about to leave and said that he had an appointment with someone else in the evening, Michiko again said *Uso.* Mr. Lerner ran out of patience and said sternly

*Uso-ja arimasen. Hontoo-desu.*
(It's not a lie. It's true.)

Michiko looked surprised and didn't seem to understand why he was so angry.

\*　　　\*　　　\*

The word *uso* by itself means "a lie" as in *uso-o tsuku* (to tell a lie), but Michiko used it not in its original sense, but simply as a response meaning "Is that right?" The word has lost its original meaning and is used merely as a substitute for *Soo-desu-ka* in this case. This use of *uso* seems to have started recently among young people, especially young women. Some young women use it quite often. They usually use it with other young people, but sometimes they inadvertently use it with older people and shock them.

This reminds us that some 10 years ago we often heard older people criticize young people for using

*Honto.* ほんと。(**True.**)

in place of *Soo-desu-ka* or *Soo*. They argued that *Honto* is impolite because it implies distrust toward the other's statement. But now this expression is used fairly widely in familiar conversations, not only by young people but also by middle-aged people.

We cannot know the future, but this *Uso* may become as popular as *Honto* just as *Honto* has outlived older people's criticism.

## 'Soba'-to 'soba'
## 「そば」と「そば」
### ('Soba noodles' and 'neighborhoods')

A new neighbor moved next door to Mr. Lerner recently. Yesterday evening this neighbor came to see Mr. Lerner and said

*Kondo otonari-e koshite-kita mono-desu.*
(I've moved into the house next door.)

while handing him an envelope. Mr. Lerner told him his name and said *Doozo yoroshiku* (Glad to meet you), and opened the envelope after the neighbor left. There were three tickets in it for *soba* at a *soba* shop nearby. The new neighbor seemed to be treating him to *soba*.

This morning Mr. Lerner asked Miss Yoshida about it. She said that there is a custom of giving *soba* to the neighbors when one moves; this is called *hikkoshi-soba* (moving soba). Do Japanese give presents not only when visiting someone, but also when moving next door to someone?

\*     \*     \*

The idea of giving *soba* to the neighbors is a pun, a play on words; *soba*, the name of a food, also means "neighborhood," so giving *soba* implies that the giver has come to the neighborhood of the receiver and wishes to stay close to him for a long time to come. (Some people say there is another meaning to it, namely that the new neighbor wants to have a relation as thin as, and as long as, *soba*.) However, this custom is becoming less popular along with changes in the relations between neighbors.

72

Japanese like to make plays on words, namely to have one word carry another meaning at the same time. *Kobu*, a kind of seaweed, is eaten on New Year's Day because it has the same pronunciation as the last part of the verb *yorokobu*, "to rejoice."

To give another example, *tai* (a kind of fish) is well-liked and used on happy occasions, not only because of its good appearance and taste, but also because of its name. *Tai* is the same sound as the last part of the word *medetai* (happy), from which the greeting *Omedetoo-gozai-masu* (Congratulations) is derived.

# *Tsukiai*
## つきあい
## (Keeping company)

The other day Mr. Lerner heard Mr. Kato ask Mr. Takada to go out drinking together after work. Mr. Kato was enthusiastic about going, but Mr. Takada wasn't. He seemed to want to go home early. Finally Mr. Kato gave up, saying

*Kimi-wa kono-goro tsukiai-ga amari yoku nai-ne.*
(You don't keep company very well these days.)

Mr. Lerner was interested in this expression. Many Japanese businessmen go to bars and restaurants to have a drink together after work for *tsukiai*. *Tsukiai* seems to be an indispensable qualification for being a good businessman in Japan.

\*          \*          \*

The word *tsukiai* is derived from the verb *tsukiau*, to keep company or to associate. *Ano-hito-towa tsukiai-ga nai* means that the speaker doesn't know someone personally. *Tsukiai-ga nagai* means that the speaker has been associated with someone for a long time.

When this word is used between members of a group as with Mr. Kato and Mr. Takada, it means involvement in the group or identification with the other members of the group. This can refer to monetary contributions too, but mostly it refers to time spent together. To be "good at *tsukiai*," one has to spend a lot of time with other members of the group. Japanese seem to like to be with other members of the group as much as possible. It does not matter whether one talks a lot or not, or whether one can amuse others or not. What counts is that one spends time with others.

This does not apply only to businessmen. Housewives belonging to the PTA are just like them. Students also feel the same way about members of the group they belong to. As long as one is good at *tsukiai*, one can be safe, even if not always happy.

*Tsukiai-da-kara shikata-ga-nai* means that one has to do something against one's will, mostly drinking, for the sake of keeping company. Drinking of this kind is called *tsukiai-zake*. つきあい酒

## *Itte-iru yoo-desu*

# 行っている　ようです

## (It seems she goes there)

When Mr. Lerner and Miss Yoshida were talking with Mr. Okada after a business discussion, Miss Yoshida remembered that Mrs. Okada had started teaching at a cooking school, and she asked Mr. Okada if she was still teaching there. Mr. Okada answered

*Ee, ima-demo itte-iru yoo-desu.*
ええ、いままでも　行っている　ようです。
(Yes, she still seems to be going there.)

Mr. Lerner wondered why he used the expression *yoo-desu* (it seems) when talking about his own wife.

After Mr. Okada had left, Mr. Lerner asked Miss Yoshida about it. She emphatically denied that Mr. and Mrs. Okada are on bad terms. She felt that the use of *yoo-desu* was just like Mr. Okada, although she couldn't explain why.

\*　　　\*　　　\*

*Yoo*, which literally means "manner," is added to sentences to mean "it seems." While *kimasu* means "he's coming" *kuru yoo-desu* means "it seems he's coming." One uses this expression when one is not sure of a fact; when one doesn't know for sure, one says *sono yoo-desu* instead of saying *soo-desu*.

However, it is up to the speaker whether he uses *yoo-desu* or not. It is possible that one speaker will use *yoo-desu* and another won't when referring to the same fact. Sometimes people choose to use *yoo-desu* even when they know a fact well, because they don't want to speak in a definite tone about it. This is often observed when people, especially men, talk about their family members in social situations; men who have higher social positions or who are self-conscious do this more often. When Miss Yoshida said that it was like Mr. Okada to use *yoo-desu*, she was referring to the fact that he is always reserved in his speech.

Very often a reserved father adds *yoo-desu* when complimented on his children. For instance, when someone praises his son's being a good baseball player and he has to admit it, he will say something like

*Ee, maa, yakyuu-wa suki-na yoo-desu.*
(Well, he seems to like baseball all right.)

# *Kyoo ikimasu*
## きょう　行きます
### (I'm coming today)

Yesterday afternoon Mr. Lerner had some business to discuss with Mr. Okada, and was going to call him to ask if it would be all right to visit his office that day. Just then Mr. Okada called, and started asking Mr. Lerner some business questions. Mr. Lerner wanted to answer his question when he visited him, so he said

*Kyoo kuru-to omoimasu.*

meaning "I think I'll come today." Then Mr. Okada asked him *Dare-ga?* (Who is?). Mr. Lerner was surprised and said *Watashi-ga* (I am). Then Mr. Okada quickly said *Aa, kite-kudasaru-n-desu-ka* (Oh, you're coming to see me?).

Miss Yoshida said that Mr. Lerner should have said

*Kyoo ikimasu.* きょう　行きます。

to mean "I'm coming today." But this didn't sound right to Mr. Lerner, because it seemed to imply that he was going away to some place other than Mr. Okada's office.

\*　　　\*　　　\*

Basic words such as *kuru* and *iku* have various usages which can't be covered easily, so we will have to limit our discussion to specific instances. In cases when the speaker and the listener are at different locations and the speaker refers to his approaching the listener, *iku* is used in

Japanese while an English speaker will say "I'm coming." In Japanese, when one goes away from where he is now, *iku* is used rather than *kuru*, regardless of whether or not one is going to where the listener is.

However, the verb *iku* is replaced by several other verbs when the speaker wants to be polite; he will use such expressions as *ukagaimasu*, *ojama-shimasu* or *mairimasu* to mean "I'm coming to where you are." So Mr. Lerner could have said *Kyoo ikimasu* as Miss Yoshida suggested, but to be more polite, he should have said *Kyoo ukagaimasu* or *Kyoo ojama-shimasu*.

When Mr. Lerner said *Kyoo kuru-to omoimasu* in the above instance, Mr. Okada didn't understand him because it sounded as if someone or something was coming either to him or to Mr. Lerner. And the use of . . . *to omoimasu* (I think . . .) sounded as if Mr. Lerner was talking about someone or something else. To imply that he couldn't say definitely that he was coming before he knew if it was all right with Mr. Okada, he could have said

> *Kyoo ojama-shitai-n-desu-ga.*
> きょう　おじゃましたいんですが。
>
> (I'd like to come today.)

# Nasake-wa hito-no tame-narazu
## なさけは　人の　ためならず
### (Kindness is not for the sake of others)

A few days ago during lunch Mr. Takada said that he had been asked by one of his friends to lend him some money and was wondering if he should do so. Then Miss Yoshida quoted a proverb

**Nasake-wa hito-no tame-narazu.**
なさけは　人の　ためならず。
(Kindness is not for the sake of others.)

Mr. Takada said that he felt the same way and that he would lend his friend as much money as he could. Miss Yoshida looked surprised and said that she had meant the opposite; she had meant that Mr. Takada shouldn't lend his friend any money.

Why did two people have quite different understandings of the same proverb? Since both Mr. Takada and Miss Yoshida seemed to believe in his or her own version, Mr. Lerner had to ask other people about it.

\*　　　\*　　　\*

Nasake-wa hito-no tame-narazu is one of the very common sayings that have been used for a long time. The literal meaning of it is "Kindness is not for the sake of others"; hito here means "other people" and narazu is the literary form meaning "isn't." The original meaning is, according to the dictionary, that to be kind toward others does good not only to the receiver, but also to the giver of the kindness. It reminds one of the famous passage from Portia's speech on mercy in Shakespeare's *The Merchant of Venice*—"it is twice blest; It blesseth him that gives and him that takes:"

Mr. Takada understood the saying in this traditional meaning, so when Miss Yoshida suggested acting in accordance with it, he thought that she was in favor of him helping his friend.

But there seems to be a new interpretation spreading among some young people; they think it means that kindness is not good for others because it will spoil them. In this sense, it is similar to the old English saying, "Spare the rod and spoil the child." Miss Yoshida believed in this interpretation, so she suggested that Mr. Takada refuse to help his friend.

# *Kaeri-de ii-kara. . .*
## 帰りで　いいから……

## (Since it's all right to buy them on your way back)

When Miss Yoshida was leaving the office to go to the post office the other day, she asked Mr. Takada if he wanted anything. He answered that he would like a pack of cigarettes if she didn't mind, and added

> *Kaeri-de ii-kara.*
> 帰りで　いいから。
> (*lit.* Since it's all right on your way back.)

Miss Yoshida nodded and left, but Mr. Lerner didn't understand why Mr. Takada had added this phrase. He asked Mr. Takada about it. Mr. Takada said that he had never thought about it and didn't know why. After that Mr. Lerner noticed that people often use phrases ending in . . . *de ii-kara* such as *ato-de ii-kara*, *chotto-de ii-kara* and the like.

\*　　　\*　　　\*

*Kaeri-de ii-kara katte-kite-kudasai* would sound strange if translated literally as "Please buy them for me since it's all right to buy them on your way back." Mr. Takada added *kaeri-de ii-kara* not as an indication of the reason why he wanted Miss Yoshida to buy him cigarettes, but as an indication of his reserve about asking her to do him a favor. This phrase can be paraphrased as follows: I hate to inconvenience you with my request, so please finish your business at the post office first without bothering with my request, and then you might pick up some ciga-·

rettes for me on your way back.

In a similar way, people often use expressions ending with . . .*de ii-kara* as in

> *Ato-de ii-kara chotto tetsudatte-kudasai.*
> あとで いいから ちょっと てつだってください。

(*lit.* Please help me a little because it's all right to do so later.)

This implies that the speaker doesn't want to inconvenience the listener by asking him to lend a hand right away.

Or, you will often hear such expressions as:

> *Chotto-de ii-kara misete-kurenai?*
> (Will you let met look at it for a moment?)

To be more formal, one sometimes uses *kekkoo-desu* for *ii* as in

> *Honno sukoshi-de kekkoo-desu-kara wakete-kudasaimasen-ka.*
> (Would you please give me a little bit of it?)

# Dekinai wake-ja arimasen-kedo. . .
## できない　わけじゃ　ありませんけど……
### (I don't mean to say that I can't but. . .)

Yesterday afternoon Mr. Lerner wanted to have some papers ready for the next day. He asked Miss Yoshida if she could type them for him. She looked through the draft and said

*Soo-desu-nee. . .* (Well,. . .)

Mr. Lerner couldn't very well force her to do it because he was rather late in getting the draft ready, so he asked her if it was impossible. She said

*Dekinai wake-ja arimasen-kedo. . .*
できない　わけじゃ　ありませんけど……
(I don't mean to say that I can't but. . .)

Mr. Lerner waited for her to complete her sentence, but it was as if she was waiting for him to say something. He sensed that she didn't want to do it very much, so he offered to do part of the typing himself and she agreed.

*　　*　　*

The expression . . .*wake-ja arimasen* (*lit.* the situation isn't that. . .) itself means "I don't mean to say that. . ." *Dekinai wake-ja arimasen-kedo* can be followed by such phrases as *kiree-ni dekinai-kamo shiremasen* (I may not be able to do it neatly) or *zangyoo-shinakereba narimasen* (I'll have to work overtime). But when . . .*wake-ja arimasen* is used with *kedo* or *ga* (but) alone, the speaker is usually implying refusal. Many

Japanese find it difficult to say "no" directly to someone's request when they want to refuse it, so they use various expressions in order to avoid saying "no"; . . .*wake-ja arimasen-kedo* is often used as one of these expressions as in

> *Dame-da-to yuu wake-ja arimasen-kedo.* . .
> だめだと いう わけじゃ ありませんけど……
> (I'm not saying no but. . .)
> *Hantai-suru wake-ja arimasen-ga.* . .
> (I don't mean to oppose you but. . .)

After these expressions, the speaker waits for the other to say something. In other words, he would rather have the request-maker take back his request on his own accord.

To avoid saying "no" to someone's request, various other expressions are used such as:

> *Sore-wa chotto.* . .
> それは ちょっと……
> (*lit.* That is a little. . .)
> *Sore-wa doo-deshoo-ne.* (I wonder about that.)
> *Ohikiuke-shitai-nowa yamayama-desu-ga.* . .
> (I would like to do it very much but. . .)

Or, *Soo-desu-nee.* . . or *Sore-wa.* . . can imply a negative answer when said with a hesitant, regretful tone.

# *Yoi kuni*

## 4192
### よ い く に

## (A good country)

Mr. Okada told Mr. Lerner and Miss Yoshida that he had recently moved and gave them his address and phone number. While writing down the phone number he said

'*Yoi kuni*'-*to oboete-kudasai*.
「よい　くに」と　おぼえてください。
(Please remember it as "a good country.")

Miss Yoshida smiled and said that it was a clever reading, but Mr. Lerner didn't understand. Miss Yoshida explained that the numbers 4-1-9-2 can be read as *yo-i-ku-ni* if the names of the numerals or the first syllables of them are combined; *yo* of *yon* (4), *i* of *ichi* (1), *ku* (9) and *ni* (2) will make up two words, *yoi* and *kuni*.

\*　　　\*　　　\*

The readings of numerals in Japanese are flexible and rich in variety, and this makes plays on words rather easy. The numerals up to 10 can be read with either readings of Japanese origin or Chinese; for example, I can be read either *hitotsu* or *ichi*, and 2 can be read either *futatsu* or *ni*. And the Japanese make use of the whole word as well as the first one or two syllables when playing on words. Thus 4-1-9-2 can be read as *yoi kuni*; some other readings may be possible but they won't be as clever as Mr. Okada's.

Such readings of phone numbers are often used for advertising a good or service. One hotel is famous for its telephone reading; its number 4-

1-2-6 is cleverly read as *yoi furo* (good bath). A maker of artificial hair (wigs) reads its phone number 341-9696 as *miyoi kuroguro*, meaning "pleasing to the eye, very black"; this must sound quite attractive to those who are losing their hair. Phone numbers which can be read with a special meaning are said to be sold and bought at high prices. On the other hand there are those who have to use unlucky numbers; someone we know is unhappy about his phone number meaning "lots of pain"; the number is 4989 so it can be read as *shiku hakku* (dire distress—*lit.* four pains and eight pains).

This kind of reading is applied not only to phone numbers but also to learning. Students often make use of this when trying to memorize numbers such as the dates of historical events; for instance 1914, the year when World War I broke out, is read as *i-ku hito-yo* (oh, those who are going away!).

# *Yoso*

## よそ

## (Other places)

A few days ago Mr. Lerner heard Mr. Takada talking over the phone with someone who was probably from some other company. It seemed that he was explaining the reason why he had to refuse that person's request. Mr. Lerner heard him say

*Yoso-wa soo-kamo shiremasen-ga . . .*
(That may be so in other companies, but . . .)

Mr. Lerner wanted to know the meaning of the word *yoso*; the dictionary says that it means "another place" or "strange place," so he guessed that Mr. Takada had used this word to mean "other companies." He wondered if this applies to places other than companies.

\* \* \*

*Yoso* is used to refer to places other than one's own; *yoso-no kaisha* means "other companies" and *yoso-no gakkoo* "other schools" as opposed to one's own company or school. In this sense *yoso-no* is different from *hoka-no* (other). The antonym for *yoso-no kaisha* is *uchi-no kaisha* as in

*Yoso-no kaisha-wa soo-kamo shiremasen-ga, uchi-no kaisha-wa chigaimasu.*
(That may be so in other companies, but not in our company.)

And *kaisha* in *yoso-no kaisha* and *uchi-no kaisha* can be left out when it is understood as in Mr. Takada's speech above, *Yoso-wa soo-kamo shiremasen-ga . . .*

Thus when one uses the word *yoso*, one is conscious of his own group as contrasted with others. A school principal may say to his students who demand to be given as much freedom as students of other schools

*Uchi-no gakkoo-wa yoso-towa chigau-n-da.*
(Our school is different from others.)

*Yoso-no hito* or *yoso-mono* means "a stranger" who has nothing to do with the speaker and the members of his group as in

*Yosomono-niwa wakaranai.*
(An outsider wouldn't understand us.)

The adjective *yoso-yoso-shii* (*lit.* like another place) describes a person behaving as if not belonging to the same group. *Yoso-yuki* or *yoso-iki* which literally means "going to some other place" usually refers to clothing, but figuratively it can refer to one's look, speech or behavior. Most people remember how excited they were to wear *yoso-iki* clothes when they were children; they also recall that they had to behave better when they wore *yoso-iki*. This is not limited to children. Most Japanese think that they have to behave differently when they leave their home and go to *yoso*.

# *Kore-ga ii-desu*

## これが　いいです

### (I want this one)

Mr. Lerner wanted to buy a tiepin for himself at a department store. The salesgirl started placing several pins one after another on the counter in front of him. He liked the first one she showed him, so he said

*Kore-wa ii-desu.*

meaning "I want this one," (*lit.* This is good), but the girl quickly moved it aside and put another one in its place, so he pointed to it and said that he wanted it. Then the girl said

*Aa, kore-ga ii-n-desu-ka.*
(Oh, you mean you want this? — *lit.* Oh, is it that this one is good?)

as if she was surprised. Mr. Lerner wondered if the difference between *ga* and *wa* can make that much difference.

\*　　　\*　　　\*

Yes, a single particle can change the meaning of a statement completely. To indicate what or which one is good, one says

**Kore-ga ii-desu.** これが　いいです。

or *Kotchi-ga ii-desu.* Similarly, to a question about which one you would like, you should say

*Kore-ga* ( or *Kotchi-ga*) *hoshii-desu.*

Or, if someone asks several people which one of them is Mr. Kato, Mr. Kato will say

*Watashi-ga Katoo-desu.*   わたしが　加藤です。

On the other hand, *wa* is used in a situation where you are asked who or how someone or something is. Mr. Kato will say *Watashi-wa Katoo-desu* when he is asked who he is; *Watashi-wa genki-desu* is used when you are asked how you are. But the phrase *watashi-wa* is not said when it is understood. Thus to the question "How are you?" one usually says *Genki-desu* instead of *Watashi-wa genki-desu*. And to introduce oneself, one usually says *Katoo-desu* rather than *Watashi-wa Katoo-desu.*

In the case of Mr. Lerner buying a tiepin mentioned above, he should have said *Kore-ga ii-desu* to mean that he wanted it. *Kore-wa ii-desu* can mean that you don't want it depending on how it is said. If you pronounce *ii-desu* strongly as

*Kore-wa II-DESU.*

it means "No, thank you." Mr. Lerner could have succeeded in conveying his desire if he had emphasized *Kore* as

*KORE-wa ii-desu.*

Or, if he had added *nee* as

*Kore-wa ii-desu-nee!*

# *Ame-ga furu-noni . . .*
## 雨が　ふるのに……
## (Although it's raining . . .)

Several people from the office planned to go on a picnic last Saturday and Mr. Lerner joined them. But when they met at the railway station it started raining. They couldn't decide for a while whether they should go or not. Mr. Lerner thought that the rain would stop pretty soon, so he said

*Ame-ga furu-noni ikimashoo.*

meaning "Let's go even though it's raining." After he said it he felt that somehow his sentence had not sounded right, so he corrected himself by saying

*Ame-ga furu-keredomo . . .*
雨が　ふるけれども……
(It's raining but . . .)

They decided to go and actually had a good time, but Mr. Lerner didn't have a chance to ask Miss Yoshida about the difference between *noni* and *keredomo.*

\*　　　\*　　　\*

*Noni* is used to indicate that what follows is against the speaker's expectation or wishes. Sentences including *noni* usually imply the speaker's regret, surprise, criticism or reprimand. *Noni* is often used in such statements as:

*Ame-ga furu-nomi pikunikku-ni iku-nante*

92

*okashii.*

(It's absurd to go on a picnic when it's raining.)

*Renshuu-shita-noni umaku narimasen.*
練習したのに　うまく　なりません。

(I don't improve although I have been practicing a lot.)

Mr. Lerner's first sentence *Ame-ga furu-noni iki-mashoo* is not appropriate because he used *noni* when making a proposal. He should have said *Ame-ga furu-keredomo . . .* or *Ame-ga futte-mo . . .* or *Ame-demo . . .* to mean "Although it's raining . . ." or "In spite of the rain . . ."

What follows *noni* is often understood and left out because *noni* has definite implications. For example, when the speaker just says

　　　*Renshuu-shita-noni . . .* (Although I practiced . . .)

the listener can guess what the speaker wants to say. A host often says to his guest who is leaving

　　　*Sekkaku oide-kudasaimashita-noni, nan-no okamai-mo shimasen-de, shitsuree-shimashita.*
　　　せっかく　おいでくださいましたのに……

(*lit.* I'm sorry I didn't do anything to entertain you when you have taken so much trouble to come.)

Very often he just says the first part and leaves the rest unsaid; bowing or some other nonverbal expression will complete the sentence.

# *Byooki*

## 病気

## (Illness)

Yesterday afternoon Mr. Lerner didn't feel well and thought that he needed some rest, so he decided to leave the office early. When he was leaving he told Miss Yoshida

*Byooki-desu-kara moo kaerimasu.*

meaning "I'm leaving now because I'm sick." She looked very concerned and insisted that she call a doctor. Mr. Lerner was surprised and told her that it was nothing serious. But she didn't understand and he had to change his words and say

*Chotto chooshi-ga warui-dake-desu.*
(I'm not feeling well; that's all.)

\*　　　\*　　　\*

Among various expressions used to indicate that one's physical condition is not good, *byooki* usually refers to rather serious illnesses that would require a doctor's treatment, and it usually takes some time before a *byooki* is cured. If you feel sick after sitting for a long time in a crowded room, for instance, you should say

*Kibun-ga* (or *Kimochi-ga*) *waruku narimashita.*
気分が　わるく　なりました。

instead of saying *Byooki-ni narimashita.* If you feel sick at seeing something very unpleasant, you should say *Kimochi-ga waruku narimashita.*

To indicate that you feel weak or very tired,

94

you should say *chooshi-ga warui* or *guai-ga warui*. *Yowai* (weak) is not used in this case; it is used to refer to peoples' constitutions rather than their conditions.

In social situations people do not describe their physical conditions or symptoms of illness too minutely, even when asked how they are. When you have caught a cold you say

*Chotto netsu-ga arimasu.* (I have a slight fever.)
or
*Samuke-ga shimasu.* (I have chills.)

but you don't say something like "my nose is running." When you have stomach trouble it is all right to say

*Onaka-no chooshi-ga warui-desu.*
(*lit.* My stomach is in poor condition.)
or
*Onaka-o kowashimashita.*
(*lit.* I have broken my stomach.)

but you shouldn't say that you have *geri* (diarrhea) or *benpi* (constipation) in social situations.

And when explaining the reason why they want to be excused, some people would just say *Chotto yooji-ga atte* . . . (I have something to do, and . . .) or *Chotto tsugoo-ga warui-node* . . . (I find it rather inconvenient, so . . .) rather than using expressions concerning their physical condition.

# Takada-san-tachi
## 高田さんたち
### (Mr. Takada and others)

Mr. Lerner was invited to Miss Yoshida's house last Saturday. When he arrived at her house she met him at the door and said

*Takada-san-tachi-mo kite-imasu.*
高田さんたちも　来ています。
(*lit.* The Takada people also came and are here.)

Mr. Lerner thought that Mr. Takada had brought his wife and children, but only Mr. Takada and his colleagues were there.

Then Mr. Lerner remembered that . . . *tachi* often means ". . . and others," and realized that Miss Yoshida had referred to Mr. Takada and others by *Takada-san-tachi*. Incidentally, he also remembered that when he first learned the word *tachi*, he made a mistake in using it; when addressing an envelope to the Takadas, he wrote

*Takada-tachi-san*

to mean "Mr. and Mrs. Takada." Miss Yoshida laughed a lot when he told her about it.

\* \* \*

*Tachi* is added to words meaning a person or to the name of a person and forms a word which indicates either that there are more than one person or that people of the same kind are included. For instance, *gakusee-tachi* can mean either "students" or "students and their like." When

96

*tachi* is added to names, it is more likely that the word indicates people of the same kind; thus *Takada-san-tachi* usually means "Mr. Takada and members of his group."

If Miss Yoshida had been referring to the Takada family, she would have said *Takada-san-to okusan-to kodomo-san-tachi* (Mr. Takada, his wife, and his children). If just Mr. and Mrs. Takada had been there, she would have said *Takada-san-to okusan*. In formal speech, one sometimes says *Takada-fusai* to mean "Mr. and Mrs. Takada."

*Tachi* can be added to pronouns for such words as *watashi-tachi* (we), *anata-tachi* (you) and *ano-hito-tachi* (they), although these words are not used as often as their English equivalents.

Another thing one has to keep in mind is that *tachi* does not imply politeness. When you want to be polite, you should use *gata* in place of *tachi* as in *anata-gata* (you), *sensee-gata* (professors), *okosan-gata* (your children) and so forth. When referring to the members of one's own group, it is modest to say *watashi-domo* instead of *watashi-tachi*.

# *Piinattsu*
## ピーナッツ
### (Peanuts)

The other day Mr. Takada brought some peanuts to the office and said that one of his relatives living in the country had sent them to him. When Miss Yoshida saw them she said that she hadn't seen any for a long time. Mr. Lerner was surprised and asked her if peanuts were so unfamiliar to her. Then she said

*Kore, piinattsu-ja nakute, nankinmame-desu-mono.*
(They aren't peanuts; they're *nankinmame*.)

*Nankinmame* is, according to the dictionary, the Japanese word for "peanuts." Mr. Takada explained taht Japanese refer to peanuts in the shell as *nankinmame*, and to shelled peanuts as *piinattsu*. ピーナッツ、なんきんまめ

\* \* \*

Sometimes the original names of things are replaced by loan words and sometimes both of them are used. When there is more than one word for one thing, people seem to want to give different meanings to the words to distinguish them. For example, both "rice" (pronounced as *raisu* in Japanese) and *gohan* are used for cooked rice. *Raisu* is used by those working at restaurants to refer to cooked rice placed on Western plates and served Western style. When referring to rice which is not cooked. Japanese use the word *kome*, but never use *raisu*; in the Japanese way of thinking, "rice" is always cooked.

The English word for *untenshu* is "driver," and this word is also used in Japanese as *doraibaa*. *Untenshu* is usually used to refer to those who drive as a profession, such as taxi drivers, train drivers, and truck drivers, while *doraibaa* usually refers to those private drivers who drive for themselves or for their families. And a similar distinction is made between Japanese and English when "drive" is used as a verb; *unten-suru* means "to drive," and *doraibu-suru* or *doraibu-ni iku* means "to go for a car drive for fun."

Sometimes even the same English word is used in two different ways in Japanese; *garasu* and *gurasu* are both derived from the English word "glass," but the former refers to glass when it is used for windows and other things, and the latter refers only to glass tumblers.

# *Warui-desu-ne*
# わるいですね
## (I'm sorry)

When Mr. Lerner was taking a walk in the vicinity of the office yesterday noon, he saw two young men playing catch in the street, perhaps making the most of their lunch time. He stood and watched them for a while. When one of the players threw the ball too high and the other had to run for it, the pitcher said

*Aa, warui, warui.*
(Sorry!—*lit.* Oh, bad, bad.)

Mr. Lerner had sometimes heard Miss Yoshida say *Warui-n-desu-kedo . . .* わるいんですけど……
(I'm sorry but . . .) but had never heard *warui* used in this way. He wondered just how many expressions Japanese use to apologize; he had learned *sumimasen, gomen-nasai, shitsuree-shimashita, mooshiwake arimasen,* but there seemed to be still more.

\*　　　\*　　　\*

*Warui* literally means "bad." It is used as an apology meaning "I shouldn't do this" or "I shouldn't have done that." *Warui-desu-ne* is used as an apology like *sumimasen,* but it is more familiar than *sumimasen.* Saying just *Warui,* like the two young men Mr. Lerner saw playing catch, is limited to very familiar conversations.

Among various expressions used for apology, *sumimasen* is used most widely; when you have to be very polite or formal you should say *Shitsuree-shimashita* or *Mooshiwake arimasen.* When

100

the speaker feels that his offense was serious, he says *Mooshiwake arimasen*. When compared with these expressions *Warui-desu-ne* sounds more familiar and casual. A father will apologize to his child saying

> *Warui-ne* or *Warukatta-ne*.
> わるいね。　わるかつたね。

A mother will say

> *Warui-wane* or *Warukatta-wane*.
> わるいわね。　わるかつたわね。

although some mothers use *gomen-nasai* more often. But a child will not say *Warui-ne* to senior members of his family. He is supposed to say *Gomen-nasai* instead.

## *Sekkaku-desu-kara. . .*
## せっかくですから……
### (Since you so kindly say so. . .)

When Mr. Lerner went to Kyoto the other day he bought a tea cup there and later presented it to Mr. Okada. Mr. Okada refused to take it at first, but when Mr. Lerner urged him again, he accepted it saying

*Sekkaku-desu-kara itadakimasu.*
せっかくですから　いただきます。

Mr. Lerner guessed that he meant he would take it since Mr. Lerner had gone to so much trouble to buy it. He was familiar with the expression *sekkaku* used with *noni* (although) as in

*Sekkaku oide-kudasaimashita-noni okamai-mo shimasen-de. . .*
(I'm sorry I didn't do anything to entertain you although you took so much trouble to come.)

He had not heard it used with *kara* as in *sekkaku-desu-kara*, and wondered how this is used.

\*　　\*　　\*

*Sekkaku* by itself means "some action has been done with special effort, and so it should be rewarded with the expected result." It is often used when the expected result has not been realized as in

*Sekkaku kai-ni itta-noni urikire-deshita.*
(I took so much trouble to go and buy it, but it was sold out.)

102

*Sekkaku katta hon-o yomu hima-ga nai.*

(I am so busy that I can't read the book that I bought.)

If Mr. Okada had not accepted his gift, Mr. Lerner might say

*Sekkaku katte-kita-noni, uketotte-kurenai.*

(I took so much trouble to buy it for him, but he wouldn't accept it.)

Thus a receiver often says *Sekkaku-desu-kara. . .* to imply that he feels he shouldn't waste the giver's kind intention and expectations.

Therefore *sekkaku-desu-kara* should be translated as "since you so kindly say so" in Mr. Okada's case. *Sekkaku-desu-kara* is used not only in such situations, but also when the speaker himself wants to make the most of his own efforts or good luck.

*Sekkaku Nihon-ni Kita-n-desu-kara. . .*
せっかく　日本に　来たんですから……
(Since I've come all the way to Japan,. . .)

implies that the speaker should do something to make the most of his being in Japan whether he has taken the trouble to come or he is just here by luck. What will come after this phrase depends on the speaker and the situation. Some people will say

. . .*sumoo-o mimashoo.* (I'll watch sumo.)
and others
. . .*sushi-o tabemashoo.* (I'll eat sushi.)
   or
. . .*Nihongo-o benkyoo-shimashoo.* (I'll study Japanese.)

103

# *Sassoku*
## さっそく
### (Right away)

Mr. Lerner has come to be able to use various expressions pretty well, but still sometimes uses them inappropriately. Just yesterday he called an electric appliance store to have them check his new TV set. He had bought it recently but somehow or other it didn't work right, so he said

*Terebi-ga sassoku kowarete-shimatta-n-desu.*

to mean "It broke right away." The man just said

*Sassoku ukagaimasu.*
さっそく　うかがいます。
(I'll come right away.)

but Miss Yoshida laughed. She said his sentence was funny because *sassoku* is used when a person is going to do something. Then Mr. Takada disagreed saying that it is all right to say

*Sassoku henji-ga kimashita.*
さっそく　返事が　来ました。
(The reply came right away.)

\*　　　\*　　　\*

Among various words meaning "soon" or "right away," *sugu* is used in many different cases. Mr. Lerner could have said *Sugu kowaremashita* and the man could have said *Sugu uka-*

104

*gaimasu*. On the other hand, *sassoku* is more limited in use; it is used when referring to a person's actions when the person is willing to do that action. Thus when someone means he will come right away to help someone else, he will say *Sassoku ukagaimasu* to imply that he is ready and willing to do so.

Therefore *Terebi-ga sassoku kowaremashita* cannot be used because a TV set has no intentions of its own. In the case of *Henji-ga sassoku kimashita*, the action of sending a reply is done by a person by his will. You cannot usually say *Sassoku ame-ga furimashita* (It rained right away) or *Sassoku kuraku narimashita* (It became dark right away) unless you're personifying nature.

You can say *Sassoku kusuri-o nomimashita* (I took the medicine right away) but you cannot say *Sassoku naorimashita* to mean "I became better very soon," because it is not within your will to become better.

# *Kesshite*
## けっして
### (Never)

Yesterday afternoon Miss Yoshida asked Mr. Lerner if he had ever been to Mr. Okada's house. She had to deliver something to him in a hurry, and wanted to know how to go there. Mr. Lerner hadn't been there, so he started to say

*lie, kesshite. . .*

meaning "Never," and then remembered that that was wrong and said

*lie, ichido-mo.* (No, not once.)

He had learned that he shouldn't say *Kesshite itta koto-ga arimasen* to mean "I haven't been there," but wondered when Japanese do use the word *kesshite*.

\*　　　\*　　　\*

*Kesshite* literally means "resolutely," so it is appropriate to use it to express one's own determination. For example, when you have decided to quit smoking, you will say

*Kesshite suimasen.*
けっして　すいません。
(I'll never smoke.)

Or, a boy who has been admonished by his teacher will say

*Moo kesshite shimasen.*
もう けっして しません。
(I'll never do it again.)

It is used not only with the speaker's determination about his future conduct, but also to express his strong belief. Thus, one can guarantee someone's good character by saying

*Ano-hito-wa kesshite warui koto-o shimasen.*
(He'd never do anything wrong.)

Or, to someone's criticism about his friend, he will protest by saying

*Ano-hito-wa kesshite warui hito-ja arimasen.*
(He's certainly not a bad person.)

Thus *kesshite* implies the speaker's determination or belief; it is not usually used to refer to what takes place naturally. For instance, it is not appropriate to say *Senshuu-wa kesshite ame-ga furanakatta* (It did not rain at all last week), since you can do nothing about rain. Instead of *kesshite* one should use here such expressions as *ichido-mo*, *sukoshi-mo* or *zenzen*.

# Nakanaka
## なかなか
## (Not easily; very)

Mr. Lerner was having dinner with the Takadas last Sunday. When he praised the cake that Mrs. Takada had made, Mr. Takada also admitted that it was good saying

*Nakanaka yoku dekita-ne.*
なかなか　よく　できたね。
(It is pretty well made.)

Then his 5-year-old son said

*Nakanaka oishii-ne.* (It's pretty good.)

Everybody laughed but Mr. Lerner didn't understand why. The word *nakanaka* is a rather difficult word. He had often heard it used but had not understood it very well. Why did they laugh when the child used it in a way similar to his father's?

\*　　　\*　　　\*

*Nakanaka* is used in two different ways in conversation. One is to mean "not easily" or "it takes a long time before. . ." For instance, when one is anxiously waiting for a bus to come, he will say

*Nakanaka kimasen-ne.*
なかなか　来ませんね。
(It's taking a long time for it to come.)

Or, when one is irritated at the low speed of recovery from illness, he may complain by saying

108

*Nakanaka naorimasen.*
(It takes a long time to get well.)

The other meaning is "very," as Mr. Takada used it to praise his wife's cake. When used to express positive evaluation, *nakanaka* implies some reserve about the praise, and the speaker often seems to be giving himself airs. Having reserve or giving oneself airs is not like a little child, so the Takadas laughed when their little son said *Nakanaka oishii-ne.* A little child would say in such a situation *Totemo oishii* (It's very good) or *Sugoku oishii* (It's terrific).

*Nakanaka* is used in the sense of "pretty" or "very" mostly by adults, and more often by men than by women, probably because of its implication of a reserved attitude.

# Sono yoo-desu
## その　ようです
### (It seems to be so)

A few weeks ago Mr. Lerner and his colleagues went to a restaurant near the office and had lunch together. After returning to the office, Miss Yoshida said that the restaurant was cheaper than any other in the neighborhood, and everyone agreed saying *Soo-desu-ne*, but Mr. Kato said

> *Sono yoo-desu-ne.*
> その　ようですね。
> (It seems to be so.)

Mr. Lerner wondered why only Mr. Kato had used *yoo-desu* when everybody had the same experience. After that he paid special attention to the way Mr. Kato talked and noticed that he used *yoo-desu* more often than anyone else in the office.

\* \* \*

The general explanation is that *yoo-desu* is used when the speaker is not sure of a fact. For instance, when someone has asked you whether your friend is also coming to the party, if you are sure he is coming, you will say

> *Ee, kimasu.* (Yes, he's coming.)

and if you are not sure, you will say

> *Ee, kuru-yoo-desu.*
> (Yes, it seems that he will come.)

110

But this explanation does not work in the case mentioned above because Mr. Kato must have noticed that the restaurant was cheaper than the others and he still used *yoo-desu*. Therefore the explanation should be revised to *yoo-desu* is used when the speaker wants to avoid sounding sure or wants to sound reserved. The use of *yoo-desu* concerns the speaker's attitude rather than his knowledge of a fact.

Yoo-desu is used when expressing one's opinion or judgment. It is not used when stating an obvious fact. It would sound strange or funny to say something like

> *Ichi tasu ichi-wa ni-ni naru yoo-desu.*
> (It seems that one and one make two.)

To the question "Is Mr. Yamamoto going?" someone will say

> *Iku-to omoimasu.* (I think he's going.)

And some will say

> *Iku yoo-ni omoimasu.*
> 行く ように 思います。
> (*lit.* I think he seems to be going.)

even when he knows that Mr. Yamamoto is going, in order to sound reserved.

# *Ee, chotto*
# ええ、ちょっと
## (Yes, a little bit)

Last Sunday Mr. Lerner visited the Takadas and was talking with Mr. and Mrs. Takada in their guest room. Then Kyoko, their 10-year-old daughter, came to the door and said

*Okaasan, chotto.*
(Will you come here for a moment, please, Mom? — *lit.* Mom, a little bit.)

Mrs. Takada said to her *Nanika yoo?* (Do you want something, dear?) while still sitting down. Kyoko opened the door a little and said

*Ee, chotto.* ええ、ちょっと。
(*lit.* Yes, a little bit.)

obviously wanting to talk to her mother alone. Mrs. Takada looked at the two men, and then stood up and left the room, saying

*Ja, chotto.*
(*lit.* Then, a little bit.)

meaning "Well then, excuse me a moment."

\*　　　\*　　　\*

The word *chotto* is used very often in daily conversation, and what follows this word is often left out as can be seen in the utterances of Mrs. Takada and her daughter above. (A general explanation of this word is given in *Nihongo Notes 1*, pp. 96-97.) *Chotto* alone is used when someone

112

wants to be excused for a while or when one wants to call someone out of the room. If the meaning is clearly understood from the situation or from some nonverbal expression like standing up or bowing. *Chotto* alone can mean *Chotto kite-kudasai* (Please come here for a moment), *Chotto shitsuree-shimasu* (Excuse me a moment) as well as many other things.

As Kyoko used it when speaking to her mother, *Ee, chotto* is used when the speaker says something with reserve or reluctantly. For example, when asked

> *Ashita-wa tsugoo-ga warui-n-desu-ka.*
> (Is tomorrow inconvenient for you?)

you will admit it regretfully saying

> *Ee, chotto.* (Yes, kind of.)

Or, when someone has noticed that you look cold and expresses his concern by asking *Samui-desu-ka* (Are you cold?), you might say

> *Ee, chotto.*

even if you are very cold, in order to sound reserved.

You may have noticed a very common exchange between two neighbors:

> A: *Odekake-desu-ka.* (*lit.* Are you going out?)
> B: *Ee, chotto.* (*lit.* Yes, a little bit.)

Neighbor A actually means something like "How are you? I hope you'll have a good time," and B actually means "Thank you. I will."

# *Oisogashii tokoro-o. . .*
## おいそがしい　ところを……
## (When you're so busy. . .)

Last Sunday afternoon Mr. Lerner visited Professor Takahashi to talk with him about the translation of his research. After an hour's discussion, the Takahashis asked him to have dinner with them. When he was leaving, he thanked Mrs. Takahashi for the meal and she thanked him for coming with a very polite expression starting with

*Oisogashii tokoro-o. . .*
おいそがしい　ところを……
(*lit.* the place where you are busy. . .)

Mr. Lerner didn't quite understand the use of the phrase *oisogashii tokoro-o*. It was Sunday and actually he didn't have much to do. Did Mrs. Takahashi say it just for formality's sake?

*　　*　　*

The phrase . . . *tokoro* refers to the situation; *yasunde-iru tokoro* means "while someone is taking a rest," and *oisogashii tokoro* means "while you're busy." The particle *o* is added to indicate the sense of "in spite of" or "regardless of." Thus *oisogashii tokoro-o wazawaza oide-kuda-saimashite* means "you took the special trouble to come to see us although you're so busy." This phrase is used as a polite expression to greet a visitor whether personal or public.

In a public meeting, for instance, the master of ceremonies will usually say something like

*Honjitsu-wa oisogashii tokoro-o tasuu oatsu-mari-itadakimashite. . .*

(I'm very happy that so many of you came to join us when you must be very busy.)

Not only the host uses this expression, but the visitor also often apologizes for taking the host's time, saying

*Oisogashii tokoro-o ojama-shimashita.* (I'm sorry I took your time.) (In this expression *to-koro-o* is used as the object of the verb *ojama-suru.*)

The underlying idea for this is that it is polite to presume that the listener must be busy and the speaker should feel guilty for causing him extra trouble.

In a similar way, one often says to someone who is going out

*Odekake-no tokoro-o sumimasen-ga. . .*
おでかけの　ところを　すみませんが……

(I'm sorry to trouble you when you're going out, but. . .)
  or
*Oisogi-no tokoro-o. . .*
おいそぎの　ところを……

(When you're in a hurry. . .)

Or, one often says to someone who has just finished work or returned from a trip

*Otsukare-no tokoro-o. . .*
おつかれの　ところを……

(When you must be tired. . .)

# Okottari shimasen
## おこったり　しません
### (I won't get angry)

Mr. Lerner and his colleagues were watching TV during their lunch hour a few days ago. When they heard the news of an actor's marriage, someone remembered that Miss Yoshida was one of his ardent fans. Mr. Takada teased her, as he often did, talking about her shock and so forth. Mr. Lerner thought that Mr. Takada had teased her too much and told him that she must be angry. Miss Yoshida heard this and said with a smile that she was used to his teasing, and added

*Watashi, okottari shimasen-yo.*
わたし、おこったり　しませんよ。
(I won't get angry.)

Mr. Lerner felt relieved, but wondered why she had said *okottari shimasen* instead of *okorimasen*. He thought that . . .*tari* . . . *tari suru* was used to indicate two or more actions.

\*　　　\*　　　\*

The . . . *tari* . . . *tari suru* form is used to indicate two or more actions that describe a state of being. For instance, *tabetari nondari shimashita* (they ate and drank) is used in order to describe how they had a good time or how they spent all their money. To describe how you spent your weekend you will say

*Eega-o mitari, kaimono-o shitari shimashita.*
映画を　見たり、買い物を　したり　しました。
(I saw a movie, did some shopping, and

116

things like that.)

You can't use . . . *tari* to connect two actions that simply take place in succession or at the same time without describing a state.

*Eega-o mitari uchi-e kaettari shimashita.*

sounds strange. You can, however, say

*Eega-o mitari shite, uchi-e kaerimashita.*
映画を　見たりして、うちへ　帰りました。
(I saw a movie, did things like that, and then went home.)

As can be seen in the example above, one often just mentions one action and leaves others unsaid when the listener can understand them. A teacher may scold his student by saying either *Okurete-wa ikemasen* (Don't be late) or *Okuretari shite-wa ikemasen* (Don't be late or do things like that). Miss Yoshida said *okottari shimasen* to mean that she wouldn't take Mr. Takada's teasing seriously, and that she wouldn't get angry or have ill feeling against him.

When one doesn't want to give various reasons, one often uses this form as in

*Kodomo-ga byooki-ni nattari shita-node. . .*
(My child became sick and other things happened, so . . .)

to apologize, for instance, for delay in paying a debt.

# *Mata kondo*
# また　こんど
## (Some other time)

Mr. Lerner wanted to buy a pearl necklace for his sister and asked Miss Yoshida to go shopping with him to help him select one. After looking for some time for a good one at one store, he decided to go to another store. But he couldn't find an appropriate expression to use to the saleswoman there who was very eager to sell them a necklace. Then Miss Yoshida said to her

*Mata kondo-ni shimasu.*
また　こんどに　します。
(We'll come again. — *lit.* I'll make it some other time.)

and left the store quickly. Mr. Lerner was relieved and thought he had to learn this expression.

\* \* \*

It is rather difficult to tell a salesman that you're not going to buy the merchandise that he has shown you. One usually doesn't say directly that he doesn't like it. Among several indirect expressions used to say that one doesn't want to buy something, *Mata kondo-ni shimasu* is very common. *Mata* literally means "again," and *kondo* means "next time"; *mata kondo* actually means "some other time." This expression is used when the speaker wants to refuse something. When someone asks you to try something, for instance, horse-riding, and you don't feel like trying it, you might use this expression. *Kono tsugi* is sometimes used in place of *kondo*, as in *Mata kono tsugi-ni shimasu.*

There are several other expressions that you can use when you leave a store without buying anything. It is important to use them with the proper timing; you should start saying them when the salesman seems to have finished talking. You can say

*Ja, moo ichido kangaete-mimasu-kara.*
(Well, I'll think it over. — *lit.* Then I'll think once more and see, so. . .)

or thank the salesman first and add that you'll think it over as in

*Doomo arigatoo. Mata. . .*
or
*Doomo sumimasen-deshita. Mata. . .*

Or you might simply thank him and leave without telling him that you're coming back some other time.

Some people leave without saying anything, but many people choose one of these expressions or just say *Doomo.* And it is customary that the salesman won't ask you again, though he may not look very happy about it.

# Oree
## お礼
### (Expression of gratitude)

The other day Miss Yoshida asked Mr. Lerner if he could help her with her English. Mr. Lerner was busy at that time, so he asked Miss Winters to help in his place. Yesterday afternoon Miss Yoshida came to thank him in this matter, and asked him

> *Ano, Wintaazu-san-ni oree-o. . .*
> あの、ウィンターズさんに　お礼を……
> (*lit.* My gratitude toward Miss Winters. . .?)

Mr. Lerner thought that Miss Yoshida wanted to know if she should thank her directly or through him, so he said *Doozo jibun-de. . .* (Please go ahead and do it yourself). Miss Yoshida looked embarrassed and again asked him

> *Demo, ikura-gurai-deshoo.*
> (How much should it be?)

\*　　　\*　　　\*

The word *oree* is used in two ways; *oree-o yuu* means to thank someone verbally, and *oree-o suru* means to give someone money or something else as payment. Miss Yoshida was referring to the second meaning while Mr. Lerner was thinking about the first meaning in the instance above. (Incidentally, *o* is an honorific prefix and *ree* itself carries the meaning, but the combined form *oree* is usually used in present-day conversation.)

To refer to a fee, one usually says *ryookin*,

but for some occupations one often uses *oree* in place of *ryookin*. For instance, one gives *oree* to teachers, doctors, lawyers and others, especially when one thinks the service has been done personally rather than as business. To refer to payments for private lessons, for instance, in foreign languages or the arts, many people use *oree* rather than *gessha* (monthly payment to teachers).

When giving money or something to express one's gratitude, one usually says

*Oree-no shirushi-ni. . .*
お礼の　しるしに……
(as a token of my gratitude. . .)

It is polite to say

*Shitsuree-desu-ga. . .* (*lit.* It's rude, but. . .)

first and then state that you're giving it to him to thank him. And if the present is money, whether cash or check, it is polite to put it in an envelope.

# Taishita koto-wa arimasen
## たいした　ことは　ありません
### (It's nothing)

When everyone was getting ready to leave the office yesterday evening, Mr. Takada was still working busily. He had something he had to finish that day. Mr. Lerner expressed his sympathy for him by saying *Taihen-desu-ne* (It's rough, isn't it?). Then Mr. Takada replied

*Iie, taishita koto-wa arimasen.*
いいえ、たいした　ことは　ありません。
(No, it's nothing.)

Mr. Lerner remembered that he had always been saying *Iie* or *Iie, daijoobu-desu* (No, it's all right) in this kind of situation, and thought he should use this expression next time.

*　　　*　　　*

*Taishita koto-wa arimasen* literally means "It's not anything of great extent"; it is used to deny that something is of high degree. For instance, when someone asks you if the play you saw was good, you might say *Taishita koto-wa arimasen-deshita* to mean "It wasn't very good." In daily conversation, one of its frequent usages is to respond to someone's expression of sympathy as in the instance above. One uses this expression not only for work, but also when referring to sickness or fatigue, as in

A: *Taihen-deshita-ne. Otsukare-deshoo.*
(That was tough. You must be tired.)
B: *Iie, taishita koto-wa arimasen. Goshinpai-*

*naku.*
(No, it's nothing. Please don't worry.)

This expression is also used for responding to someone's compliment like

*Nihongo-ga ojoozu-desu-ne.*
(You speak Japanese very well.)

You can deny it by saying something like

*Iie, sonna koto-wa arimasen.*
(No, it's no such thing.)
or
*Iie, tondemo arimasen.*
(No, not at all.)

But these are complete denial. When you have to admit the truth of the compliment to some extent, you can say *Iie, taishita koto-wa arimasen* (No, I'm not very good) or *Sorehodo-demo arimasen* (*lit.* It's not to the extent you say).

# *Konna jikan-ni sumimasen*
## こんな　時間に　すみません
### (I'm sorry to trouble you at such an hour)

Mr. Okada called Mr. Lerner at his office yesterday afternoon around five o'clock. He started by saying

*Konna jikan-ni sumimasen-ga. . .*
こんな　時間に　すみませんが……
(*lit.* I'm sorry at such an hour, but. . .)

Mr. Lerner said that he didn't mind at all, but it took him some time to realize that Mr. Okada was sorry for calling him when he must be getting ready to leave the office. He remembered that many Japanese start talking on the phone with an apology of some kind or other. He wished he had listened to them more carefully so that he could use such apologies himself.

\*　　　\*　　　\*

The basic form of apology is *. . .te sumimasen* as in *osoku natte sumimasen* (I'm sorry I'm late). The whole sentence should be, in Mr. Okada's utterance above, *Konna jikan-ni denwa-shite sumimasen* (I'm sorry to call you at such an hour); *denwa-shite* is understood and left out.

It is polite to apologize for disturbing someone by calling him at an inconvenient time, although it is rather difficult to know what time would be convenient for the listener. Usually at an early hour one says

*Konna-ni asa hayaku sumimasen.*
こんなに　朝　はやく　すみません。

(Sorry to call you at such an early hour as this in the morning.)

And late at night one says

*Konna-ni yoru osoku sumimasen.*
こんなに　夜　おそく　すみません。
(Sorry to call you at such a late hour as this at night.)

In both of these sentences *Konna-ni* can be left out. At mealtime one says

*Oshokuji-no jikan-ni.* . . ( . . .at mealtime.)

And in all these instances, one can say

*Konna jikan-ni.* . . ( . . .at such an hour.)

These expressions are used not only when telephoning but also when visiting someone. There are several other common expressions for apologizing for disturbing someone at an inconvenient time. Some expressions have *tokoro-o* (while) as in *oisogashii tokoro-o* (when you're busy) or *oyasumi-no tokoro-o* (when you're resting). (See pp. 114-115.) There are some other expressions with *chuu* (in the midst of) as in *oshigoto-chuu* (when you're at work), *oshokuji-chuu* (when you're eating) or *gobenkyoo-chuu* (when you're studying). When you have to interrupt someone engaged in conversation with someone else, you can say *Ohanashi-chuu sumimasen-ga* (I'm sorry to interrupt you when you're talking with someone).

# *Konna kanji-ni shite-kudasai*
# こんな 感じに してください
### (Please make it like this)

Mr. Lerner went into a barber shop yesterday afternoon. When he sat down, he noticed a picture showing a man with a hair style which he liked, so he pointed to it and told the barber

*Kono katachi-ni shite-kudasai.*
(Please cut my hair in this shape.)

The barber understood and started cutting his hair. Then a young man came in and sat next to him. He also pointed to the picture and said

**Konna kanji-ni onegai-shimasu.**
こんな 感じに おねがいします。
(Please do it like this.)

Mr. Lerner knew the word *kanji*, but did not know that it could be used in this way.

\* \* \*

The word *kanji* by itself means "feeling" or "impression." *Kanji-no ii hito* means "a pleasant person" or "an agreeable person" (*lit.* a person who gives a good impression). *Donna kanji-no hito* means "what type of person?" A barber or a hairdresser will often ask the customer

*Donna kanji-ga yoroshii-desu-ka.*
(*lit.* What kind of impression will be good?)

meaning "What style would you like?" And if the customer wants the barber or hairdresser to follow a certain model, he says

*Konna kanji-ni shite-kudasai* or . . .*onegai-shimasu.*
こんな　感じに　してください。

Incidentally, *koo-yuu* is also used to mean "this kind of." *Koo-yuu*, *soo-yuu*, *aa-yuu*, and *doo-yuu* sound a little more formal than *konna*, *sonna*, *anna* and *donna.*

It is grammatically correct to say *Kono ka-tachi-ni shite-kudasai* as Mr. Lerner said. Or some people say while showing an instruction

*Kono toori-ni shite-kudasai.*
(Please do it just as this says.)

These sentences are correct but sound as if you want the listener to try very hard to be exact, and therefore they sound demanding or imposing. It is regarded as considerate to show reserve about your request by using such expressions as

*konna kanji* (this kind of impression)
*konna fuu* (this kind of fashion) or,
*konna guai* (this kind of manner).

# *Jimejime-shite iya-desu-ne*
## じめじめして　いやですね
### (It's humid and unpleasant, isn't it?)

Mr. Okada seems to like to talk about the weather very much, so Mr. Lerner wanted to be able to talk about it, too. Just yesterday, he learned several words from the dictionary before he met Mr. Okada. It had been raining for several days so he said *Shitsudo-ga takai-desu-ne* (The humidity is high, isn't it?). When Mr. Okada was leaving, the weather seemed to be starting to improve, so he said *Ashita-wa kaisee-deshoo* (Tomorrow will be a fine day). Mr. Okada readily agreed.

But after Mr. Okada left, Miss Yoshida, who had been with them, said that Mr. Lerner had sounded like an announcer giving the weather forecast. She said that the sentences he had used were correct but not conversational. For humid weather he should have said

*Jimejime-shite iya-desu-ne.*
じめじめして　いやですね。
(It's humid and unpleasant, isn't it?)

and for anticipating a clear day, he should have said

*Ashita-wa karari-to* (or *karatto*) *hareru-de-shoo.*
あしたは　からりと　晴れるでしょう。

\*　　　\*　　　\*

There are many onomatopoeic words and other expressions used for describing weather or cli-

128

mate in Japanese. On wet and unpleasant days one often uses such expressions as *jime-jime-shite-iru* and *shimeppoi* to mean "damp" or "humid." And when the temperature is also high, one says *mushiatsui*; *mushi* stands for "steam" and *atsui* for "hot."

When it has cleared up and the air feels pleasant because it is not humid any more, one uses *karari-to* or *karatto* as in

*Karatto-shite kimochi-ga ii-desu-ne.*
(It's fine and it feels nice.)

During the rainy season which usually lasts for about one month from mid-June to mid-July, one often talks about the rain. To mention a few of the many expressions used for describing rain, when it rains heavily one says

*Zaazaa futte-imasu.* (It's pouring.)

When fine drops of rain fall quietly and softly, one says

*Shitoshito futte-imasu.* (It's raining quietly.)

And to describe the rain when it starts falling lightly as if scattering here and there, one says

*Parapara furidashimashita.*
(It has started sprinkling.)

The word *parapara* describes the light sound that is made by the rain hitting things.

# Ippai nomu
## いっぱい のむ
### (To have a drink)

Mr. Lerner and Mr. Takada were going out together to visit someone yesterday afternoon, and as Mr. Lerner was getting ready to leave the office Miss Yoshida came to him and asked if he would like a cup of coffee. Mr. Lerner wanted to have some, so he called out to Mr. Takada, who was talking with someone in another corner of the room. Mr. Lerner said in a loud voice

*Ippai nonde-kara ikimashoo.*
(*lit.* Let's go out after we've had a cup.)

Before Mr. Takada could answer, everyone in the room looked at Mr. Lerner and Miss Yoshida laughed.

\*　　　\*　　　\*

To count liquids in a cup or glass, one uses such counter words as *ippai* (one cup), *nihai* (two cups), *sanbai* (three cups), etc.; *hai* or *pai* or *bai* stands for a cup or glass. These counter words are used as in

*Ocha-o sanbai nomimashita.*
お茶を　さんばい　のみました。
(I had three cups of tea.)
*Koohii-o ippai nomimashoo.*
コーヒーを　いっぱい　のみましょう。
(Let's have a cup of coffee.)

But when one just says *ippai nomimashita* without specifying what one drank, it usually means that the speaker had some alcoholic beverage. Thus Mr. Takada thought that Mr. Lerner was going with him after having some beer or sake or other alcoholic beverage. If someone invites you, saying

*Ippai nomi-ni ikimashoo-ka.*

it means that he wants to have some alcoholic beverage with you.

In this usage, *ippai* does not necessarily mean just one glass; *ippai* actually stands for "some" or "little."

There are other words with "one" meaning "some." *Hito-yasumi* which literally means "one rest" actually means "resting awhile" as in

*Kono hen-de hito-yasumi shimasen-ka.*
(Shall we take a rest now?)

Several other expressions with *hito-* are often used in daily conversation. *Hito-nemuri* (sleeping awhile), *hito-shigoto* (a unit of work) and *hito-furo* (a bath) are a few examples.

The word *hitotsu* (one) is often used for proposing or offering something as in

*Hitotsu ikaga-desu-ka.*
ひとつ　いかがですか。
(Won't you have some?)
*Hitotsu tameshite-kudasai.* (Please try it.)

Saying *hitotsu ikaga-desu-ka* doesn't necessarily mean that the speaker wants you to have just one; you can go ahead and have several.

# *Tasukarimashita*
## たすかりました
### (You helped me)

Miss Yosida was busy working all day yesterday, and it seemed she would be unable to finish her work by five o'clock. Mr. Lerner found some time to help her so that she could finish her work earlier. When the work was finished she thanked him and added

*Hontoo-ni tasukarimashita.*
ほんとうに　たすかりました。
(You really helped me.)

Mr. Lerner remembered that he had often wanted to say something nice when someone helped him and had wished he knew some expression other than *Arigatoo-gozaimashita*. He also remembered that once he had said *Tasukemashita* to mean "You helped me," but it hadn't seemed to work.

*　　*　　*

The word *tasukaru* means "to be helped" while *tasukeru* means "to help someone." Saying *Tasukemashita* sounds as if the listener had helped someone other than the speaker. When one wants to thank someone for his help, one should use *Tasukarimashita* to mean "You helped me."

This expression can also be used when a third person has helped the speaker as in

*Tomodachi-ga tetsudatte-kureta-node tai-hen tasukarimashita.*

(My friend lent me a hand, so I was helped a great deal.)

Sometimes people feel that they are helped by nature. For instance when it has become pleasantly cool after serial hot days, they say

*Kyoo-wa suzushikute tasukarimasu-ne.*
きょうは　すずしくて　たすかりますね。
(Today's nice and cool, so it helps us a great deal.)

When someone has thanked you for your help by saying *Tasukarimashita*, you can either simply say *Iie*, or *Iie, doo-itashimashite* (You're welcome — lit. Far from it . . .). More politely you can say

*Iie, taishita oyaku-ni tachimasen-de . . .*
(No, I'm afraid I wasn't much help.)
*Iie, nanno oyaku-nimo tachimasen-de . . .*
(No, I'm afraid I wasn't any help.)

# *Doozo goyukkuri*
## どうぞ　ごゆっくり
### (Please make yourself at home)

Mr. Lerner visited Mr. Okada at his office last Friday on business. While they were discussing some matter Mr. Sato, the director of the company, came into the room to meet Mr. Lerner. After they exchanged *Doozo yoroshiku* (How do you do?), Mr. Sato left the room; as he was leaving he said to Mr. Lerner

> *Doozo goyukkuri.*
> どうぞ　ごゆっくり。
> (*lit.* Please take your time.)

Mr. Lerner thanked him because it sounded like an expression of hospitality, but he wondered what it meant exactly.

*　　*　　*

*Doozo goyukkuri* means not only "take your time" but also "please be relaxed" when used as an indication of hospitality. This is usually said to a visitor of someone in one's family.

Suppose you visit a married woman at her home. While you're talking with her, her husband will come into the room to meet you or to say hello to you. Usually he will greet you with

> *Irasshai.* いらっしゃい。 (Welcome.)

or more politely, *Yoku irasshaimashita.*

You, as a visitor, will say

*Ojama-shite-imasu.*
おじゃましています。

which literally means ''I'm disturbing your home,'' but actually corresponds to ''hello, how are you?''

When leaving after talking awhile, the husband will say to you

*Doozo goyukkuri.*

This is an expression of welcome to a visitor said by a representative of a household or organizations such as companies. Either husband or wife will say this, but a maid or young member of the family will not usually say it. At companies, it is proper for the director or someone superior to the receiver of the visitor to say it, but one does not usually say it to someone who is visiting his superior.

# Tekitoo-ni yatte-kudasai
## てきとうに やってください
### (Please use your own judgment)

While Mr. Lerner and Mr. Takada were talking during a break in their work, Miss Yoshida
came to ask Mr. Takada some questions about
the typing he had asked her to do. Mr. Takada
answered several specific questions, and then
said

**Ato-wa tekitoo-ni yatte-kudasai.**
あとは てきとうに やってください。
(*lit.* As for the rest, please do it properly.)

Miss Yoshida said that she understood and left
them. Mr. Lerner wondered what the expression
*tekitoo-ni* means exactly, and also wondered
why she had gone back to her work without asking any further questions.

\*　　　\*　　　\*

The word *tekitoo* usually means "appropriate," as in such expressions as *tekitoona kotoba*
(appropriate words) or *tekitoona hito* (suitable
person). But in a situation as mentioned above,
*Tekitoo-ni yatte-kudasai* or *Tekitoo-ni onegai-
shimasu* means "Please do it in the way you
think is appropriate," and actually implies that
the speaker leaves it to the judgment of the listener.

Suppose someone asks you to plan a party to
celebrate the anniversary of the founding of the
company, and tells you the amount of money you
can spend and the names of the people to be invited. When you ask him what portion of money

should go for drinks and what portion for food, he
may say

*Sore-wa tekitoo-ni yatte-kudasai.*
それは　てきとうに　やってください。

meaning that the matter is left to you.

There still remains a question as to what extent you can use your own judgment. When
saying *tekitoo-ni* the speaker usually has some
idea of how the work should be carried out, and
doesn't expect you to do things in a way completely different from his idea. You will check
the previous cases and try not to deviate too
much from them.

Thus the expression *tekitoo-ni* can be used in
this way only in situations where the speaker and
the listener share the same understanding. Even
among Japanese sometimes the listener has a difficult time sensing what the speaker actually expects of him. And this expression is usually used
by a speaker to someone who is not superior to
him because it is impolite for him to expect his
superior to sense his intentions.

# *Hareru yoona ki-ga shimasu*
## 晴れる　ような　気が　します
### (I have a feeling it's going to clear up)

It was raining hard yesterday morning but by lunchtime it wasn't raining as hard. Someone wondered if it would keep raining through the evening. Mr. Takada said

> *Kyoo-wa furu-to omoimasu-ne.*
> (I think it will rain all day today.)

Then Miss Yoshida disagreed, saying

> **Watashi-wa hareru yoona ki-ga shimasu-kedo.**
> わたしは　晴れる　ような　気が　しますけど。
> (*lit.* I have a feeling that it will clear up, but.)

Mr. Lerner had heard the expression . . . *ki-ga suru* before, but now he thought about the difference between . . . *to omou* and . . . *yoona ki-ga suru*, and wondered which sounds more definite.

*　　*　　*

There are various expressions with *ki* such as *ki-ga suru*, *ki-ni naru*, *ki-ga tsuku*, etc. *Ki-ga suru* literally means "I have a feeling," and sometimes is added to adjectives as in *iyana ki-ga suru* (I feel it's unpleasant), *zannenna ki-ga suru* (I feel it's regrettable), or *donna ki-ga shimasu-ka* (how do you feel about it?). But the more common usuage is to express one's opinion in a reserved way and for this purpose it usually follows *yoona* as in *hareru yoona ki-ga suru*. Saying . . . *yoona ki-ga suru* sounds less definite than . . . *to omou*. For instance, when discussing whether someone is coming, saying

> *Kyoo kuru-to omoimasu.*
> (I think he will come today.)

sounds as if the speaker has some reason to believe that the person will come, while saying

> *Kyoo kuru yoona ki-ga shimasu.*
> きょう 来る ような 気が します。

implies that the speaker doesn't have any definite reason to think so.
　Very often *nan-to-naku* (for no particular reason) is used with *ki-ga suru* as in

> *Nan-to-naku kyoo kuru yoona ki-ga shimasu.*

　Since this expression implies that the speaker does not have any particularly sound reason, it is used when expressing one's opinion in a reserved way. For instance, when politely criticizing someone's plan, you might say

> *Amari yaku-ni tatanai yoona ki-ga shimasu.*
> (I have a feeling it won't be very useful.)
> 　or
> *Doomo amari yoku nai yoona ki-ga shimasu.*
> (I have a feeling it isn't so good.)

And *ki-ga suru* is used when agreeing with someone, as in

> *Ee, sonna ki-ga shimasu-ne.*
> (Yes, I feel that way, too.)

139

# Kowashite-arimasu
## こわしてあります
### (Someone has broken it)

Mr. Lerner recently learned a new grammatical rule: he was told that a transitive verb plus *te-arimasu* means the same thing as an intransitive verb plus *te-imasu*; namely, both *mado-ga akete-arimasu* and *mado-ga aite-imasu* mean "the window is open." He wanted to use this expression in actual conversation some time. Yesterday morning when he tried to turn on the reading lamp on his desk at the office, he noticed that it didn't work, so he showed it to Miss Yoshida and told her

   *Kowashite-arimasu-ne.*

to mean "it's broken." He thought that was just the same as *Kowarete-imasu-ne*, but Miss Yoshida didn't understand. She said that he should say *Kowarete-imasu-ne* instead.

*       *       *

It is often explained as a grammatical rule that the two expressions — a transitive verb plus *te-arimasu* and an intransitive verb plus *te-imasu* — are used in the same way. According to this, the expressions in the two groups below mean the same thing:

   **Group 1**
   *aite-imasu* (< *aku*, v.i.)
   *shimatte-imasu* (< *shimaru*, v.i.)
   *denki-ga tsuite-imasu* (< *tsuku*, v.i.)

**Group 2**
   *akete-arimasu* (<*akeru*, v.t.) (it's open)
   *shimete-arimasu* ( < *shimeru*, v.t.) (it's closed)
   *denki-ga tsukete-arimasu* ( < *tsukeru*, v.t.) (the light is on)

It is true that the two types of expressions are used to describe the same state of things, but the speaker's mental attitude towards this state of things is different. In this sense, the two expressions should not be regarded as the same. While expressions in group 1 are used to describe the state of things just as they are, expressions in group 2 imply that someone has done the action purposely, and they often imply the speaker's surprise, criticism, reprimand, or other such feelings. Miss Yoshida didn't understand when Mr. Lerner said *Kowashite-arimasu-ne* because that implied that he was blaming someone for purposely damaging his reading lamp.

   This contrast is, however, not applied to all verbs. Some verbs do not have corresponding transitive or intransitive verbs, and sometimes the *te-arimasu* form cannot be used because the meaning would be strange. For instance, you can say *Mise-ga narande-imasu* (Several stores are line up), but you cannot say *Mise-ga narabete-arimasu* (Someone has lined up the stores).

## *Konnano-de yokattara . . .*
## こんなので よかったら……
### (If such a thing as this will do, . . .)

Yesterday evening Mr. Lerner visited Professor Takahashi and talked with him for about an hour. When he was leaving, it suddenly started to rain, but he didn't have an umbrella with him. Mrs. Takahashi brought an extra umbrella which was rather old. The professor complained about it to his wife, and then offered it to Mr. Lerner saying

*Konnano-de yokattara doozo omochi-kudasai.*
こんなので よかったら どうぞ お持ちください。
(Please use it if this one is all right. — *lit.* If such a one like this will do, please take it with you.)

Mr. Lerner politely said *Kekkoo-desu* (This is fine) and remembered to add a phrase he had recently learned, *Tasukarimasu* (It's a great help).

\*　　\*　　\*

The expression . . . *de yokattara* (if . . . will do) is used when offering something in a reserved way. If you want to say "this is an old one but I'd like you to use it," you can say

*Furuino-de yokattara*

and you can also say

*Konna furuino-de yokattara*

to mean "if you don't mind such an old one."

142

This expression is used not only when offering a physical object but also when offering one's services. If you can't help someone right away but only after some time, you can say *ato-de yokattara*.

In conferences or on formal occasions it is rather difficult for one to propose to undertake some work, especially when the work seems to be honorable or difficult in some way. You can start by saying

*Anoo, watashi-de yokattara*
あのう、わたしで よかつたら

meaning "if I'm good enough" or "if I may," and go on to say

*otetsudai-sasete-kudasai.* (please let me help you.)

Salesmen will use . . . *de yokattara* when offering a substitute when they don't have the exact merchandise the customer wants as in

*Moo sukoshi chiisaino-de yokattara arimasu-ga.*
(We have a smaller one, if you'd like it.)

And to make the expression more polite, *yoroshi-kattara* is often used in place of *yokattara*.

# Daiji-ni shite-kudasai
## だいじに　してください
### (Please treat it as important)

Yesterday noon when Mr. Lerner was leaving the office for lunch, he forgot to turn his reading lamp off. Miss Yoshida noticed it and said

*Denki-o daiji-ni shite-kudasai.*
電気を　大事に　してください。
(*lit.* Please treat the electricity as important.)

Mr. Lerner went back to his desk and turned the light off. While doing so he wondered if the expression *daiji-ni suru* in Miss Yoshida's sentence was the same as the phrase often used towards a sick person, *Doozo odaiji-ni* どうぞ　お大事に。 to mean "Please take care of yourself."

\* \* \*

The two expressions *denki-o daiji-ni suru* and *Doozo odaiji-ni* come from the same idea; *daiji-ni suru* means "to treat something as important" or "to make much of something." The set expression *Doozo odaiji-ni* is an abbreviation of *Doozo karada-o daiji-ni shite-kudasai* (Please treat your health as important). In the same way *Denki-o daiji-ni shite-kudasai* means "Please consider electricity as important and don't waste it."

*Daiji-ni suru* is often used with such things as time and money as in

*Okane-o daiji-ni shinakereba.* (We must spend our money carefully.)
*Jikan-o daiji-ni shimashoo.* (Let's spend our

144

time effectively.)

The idea of using something carefully is also expressed by the word *mottainai* (too good to waste — cf. pp. 10-11). Miss Yoshida might have admonished Mr. Lerner for having left the light on by saying

*Denki-ga mottainai-desu-yo.*
(*lit.* It's a pity to waste electricity.)

The expression *daiji-ni suru* is sometimes used with persons too. The sentence *Okusan-o daiji-ni shite-imasu* (*lit.* He treats his wife as important) roughly corresponds to the English "He loves his wife." Many Japanese, especially older people, prefer using various other expressions to using the word *ai-suru* (to love), and this *daiji-ni suru* is one such expression. A wife may say to her husband who is too busy working to be with his children,

*Motto kodomo-o daiji-ni shite-kudasai.*
(Please pay more attention to your children.)

# *Kikimasen*

## ききません

### (He won't listen to me)

A few minutes after Mr. Takada left the office on business, Miss Yoshida noticed that he had forgotten to take some papers he needed. Mr. Lerner opened the window and looked down the street, but Mr. Takada was already too far to call back, so he told her

*Moo yondemo kikimasen-yo.*

meaning "He won't hear me even if I call to him." Miss Yoshida said she would take care of the papers and thanked Mr. Lerner, and then said that he should have said

. . . *kikoemasen* きこえません。

instead of *kikimasen*. Mr. Lerner remembered that he had made this mistake before and felt that he had to study some more about it.

\*　　\*　　\*

The word *kiku* has several meanings such as "to hear," "to ask," and others; for hearing, another word *kikoeru* is also used. There is a difference between the two; *kiku* means "to hear" and *kikoeru* means "can be heard." There is another important difference in that while *kikoeru* is used to indicate that a sound is physically audible, *kiku* concerns one's intentional or habitual action of hearing something. Thus, when Mr. Lerner said *kikimasen*, it sounded as if Mr. Takada wouldn't listen to him because he didn't want to.

*Kiku* is used in these sorts of situations:

*Chittomo watashi-no yuu koto-o kikimasen.*
ちっとも　わたしの　言う　ことを　ききません。
(He won't listen to me at all.)
*Kono-goro yoku soo-yuu hanashi-o kikimasu-ne.*
(We often hear about that kind of thing nowadays.)

On the other hand, *kikoeru* is used when one can hear a sound whether he wants to or not as in

*Semi-no koe-ga kikoemasu-ne.* (We hear cicadas singing.)

Or, when you can't hear someone well on the phone, you will say

*Yoku kikoemasen.* (I can't hear you well.)
  or
*Denwa-ga tookute, yoku kikoemasen.* ( *l i t* . The telephone is far and I can't hear well.)

A similar distinction exists between *miru* (to see) and *mieru* (can be seen) as in

*Eega-o mimashoo.* (Let's see a movie.)
*Kyoo-wa Fujisan-ga miemasu.* (We can see Mt. Fuji today.)

# GUIDE FOR AVOIDANCE OF COMMON MISTAKES

The following is a list of basic grammatical items and example sentences accompanied with explanations; this is designed to help those who are studying Japanese avoid making common mistakes. Although the selection of items is based on error analysis, correct model sentences are given first and then the errors are explained later, in order not to impress the reader with wrong usages. In most of items, one or two additional examples are added for reference.

Since space is limited, the list is not a comprehensive one, but we have tried to include basic and typical items with which students are apt to have trouble.

Going through the list will help confirm your knowledge of basic Japanese grammar, and if you want further information on any of the items, we recommend that you refer to either *Nihongo Notes 1, 2 & 3* (abbreviated as NN-1, NN-2, NN-3) or *An Introduction to Modern Japanese* (abbreviated as IMJ).

1. CONNECTING TWO ADJECTIVES
a) *Hirokute shizuka-desu.* (It's spacious and quiet).

It is wrong to say: *Hiroi-to shizuka-desu.*

Additional examples:
   *Atarashikute kiree-desu.* (It's new and beautiful.)
   *Atarashikute kireena hoteru.* (A new and beautiful hotel)

(cf. IMJ, p. 59)

b) *Shizuka-de suzushii-desu.* (It's quiet and cool.)

It is wrong to say: *Shizuka-to suzushii-desu.*

Additional example:
   *Kantan-de yasashii shigoto-desu.* (It's a simple and easy work.)

You can also say:
   *Kantanna yasashii shigoto-desu.* (It's a simple and easy work.)

(cf. IMJ, p. 59)

2. NEGATIVE FORM OF *KIREE*
*Amari kiree-ja arimasen.* (It's not very beautiful.)

It is wrong to say: *Amari kireeku arimasen.*

(cf. IMJ, p. 61)

3. MEETING WITH PEOPLE
*Iroirona hito-ni aimashita.* (I met with various people.)

It is wrong to say: *Iroirona hito-o arimashita.*

It is grammatically correct but different in meaning to say: *Iroirona hito-o mimashita,* which means that you physically saw various people but didn't talk with them.

(cf. IMJ, p. 59)

4. POSITION OF A NUMBER IN A SENTENCE
*Ringo-o itsutsu kudasai.* (Please give me five apples.)

It is not appropriate to say: *Itsutsu-no ringo-o kudasai*, because it implies that you are referring to five specific apples.

Additional example:

*Hon-o sansatsu kaimashita.* ( I bought three books.)

(cf. IMJ, p. 73; NN-3, pp. 54-5)

## 5. INDICATING PURPOSE

a) *Asobi-ni kite-kudasai.* (Please come to visit me. — *lit.* Please come to have a good time.)

It is wrong to say: *Asobu-ni kite-kudasai.*

It is awkward to say: *Asobu tame-ni kite-kudasai.*

It is different in meaning to say: *Mi-ni kite-kudasai*, which sounds as if you are asking someone to come to see some object, not you.

Additional examples:

*Eega-o mi-ni ikimashoo.* (Let's go to see a movie.)

*Nanika tabe-ni ikimasen-ka.* (Won't you go to eat something?)

(cf. IMJ, p. 86)

b) *Ryokoo-ni ikimashita.* (I went on a trip.)

It is wrong to say: *Ryokoo-e ikimashita*, because *e* indicates the destination.

It is awkward to say: *Ryokoo-no tame-ni ikimashita.*

Additional example:

*Nihon-e shigoto-ni kimashita.* (I came to Japan to work.)

(cf. IMJ, p. 86)

## 6. TALKING WITH PEOPLE

*Tanaka-san-to hanashimashita.* (I talked with Mr. Tanaka.)

It is awkward to say: *Tanaka-san-to issho-ni hanashimashita.* . . . *to issho-ni* is used mainly for actions other than talking, as in *Tanaka-san-to issho-ni ikimashita.* (I went with Mr. Tanaka.)

Additional example:

*Tanaka-san-towa hanashimashita-ga, Yama-*

150

da-san-towa hanashimasen-deshita. (I talked with Mr. Tanaka, but didn't talk with Mr. Yamada.)

(cf. IMJ, p. 110)

7. DESCRIBING A STATE OF BEING WITH THE *TE-IRU* FORM
*Ano megane-o kakete-iru hito-wa dare-desu-ka.* (Who is that person wearing glasses?)

It is wrong to say: *Ano megane-o kakeru hito-wa dare-desu-ka*, because it means that the person is going to wear glasses. . . . *megane-o kaketa . . .* is also used.

Additional examples:
*Tanaka-san-wa yasete-imasu.* (Mr. Tanaka is thin.)
*Michiko-san-wa kekkon-shite-imasu.* (Michiko is married.)

(cf. IMJ, p. 98; NN-1, pp. 34-5)

8. ADVERBS IN NEGATIVE STATEMENTS
a) *Zenzen wakarimasen-deshita.* (I didn't understand it at all.)
*Sukoshi-mo wakarimasen-deshita.* (I didn't understand it at all.)

It is awkward to say: *Kesshite wakarimasen-deshita.*

It is ambiguous to say: *Minna wakarimasen-deshita.*

(cf. NN-3, pp. 106-7)

b) *Amari benkyoo-shimasen-deshita.* (I didn't study much.)

It is awkward to say: *Yoku benkyoo-shimasen-deshita.*

: *Takusan benkyoo-shimasen-deshita.*

(cf. IMJ, pp. 50, 53)

9. COMPARING TWO THINGS
*Kochira-no hoo-ga ookii-desu.* (This one is bigger.)

It is awkward to say: *Kochira-wa motto ookii-desu.*

It is appropriate to use . . . *no hoo-ga* when the statement concerns which one is bigger. When referring to something bigger than what has been mentioned before *motto ookii* is used as in: *Motto ookiino-o kudasai.* (Please give me a bigger one.)

Additional example:

*Tookyoo-no hoo-ga Kyooto-yori jinkoo-ga ooi.* (Tokyo has a larger population than Kyoto does.)

(cf. IMJ, p. 121)

10. INDICATING EXCESSIVE DEGREE

a) *Ookisugimasu.* (It's too big.)

It is awkward to say: *Amari ookii-desu.*

Additional example:

*Mada wakasugiru-deshoo.* (I'm afraid he is still too young.)

(cf. IMJ, p. 350)

b) *Nomisugite atama-ga itai.* (I drank too much and have a headache.)

It is awkward to say: *Amari nonde atama-ga itai.*

Additional example:

*Tabesugiru-to onaka-o kowashimasu.* (If you eat too much, it's bad for your stomach.)

(cf. IMJ, p. 350)

11. USE OF PLAIN FORMS WHEN REPORTING SOMEONE'S SPEECH OR WHEN STATING WHAT YOU THINK

a) *Zannen-da-to iimashita.* (He said that it was regrettable.)

*Zannen-da-to omoimasu.* (I think that it is regrettable.)

It is awkward to say: *Zannen-desu-to iimashita (omoimasu).*

Additional examples:

*Nihonjin-da-to iimashita.* (He said that he was a Japanese.)

*Watashino-da-to omoimasu.* (I think it's mine.)

(cf. IMJ, p. 97; NN-2, pp. 100-1)

152

b) *Kuru-to iimashita.* (He said that he would come.)
   *Kuru-to omoimasu.* (I think that he will come.)

   It is awkward to say: *Kimasu-to iimashita (omoimasu).*

   It is wrong to say: *Kuru-da-to iimashita (omoimasu).*

Additional examples:
   *Hataraite-iru-to iimashita.* (He said that he was working.)
   *Moo owatta-to omoimasu.* (I think that it is over now.)

                              (cf IMJ, p. 97; NN-2, pp. 100-1)

c) *Ii-to iimashita.* (He said that it was all right.)
   *Ii-to omoimasu.* (I think that it's all right.)

   It is awkward to say: *Ii-desu-to iimashita (omoimasu).*

   It is wrong to say: *Ii-da-to iimashita (omoimasu).*

                              (cf. IMJ, p. 96, NN-2, pp. 100-1)

d) *Ii-daroo-to iimashita.* (He said that it would be all right.)
   *Ii-daroo-to omoimasu.* (I think that it will be all right.)

   It is awkward to say: *Ii-deshoo-to iimashita (omoimasu).*

Additional examples:
   *Tabun soo-daroo-to iimashita.* (He said that it was probably so.)
   *Tabun kuru-daroo-to omoimasu.* (I think that he will probably come.)

                              (cf. IMJ, p. 121; NN-2, pp. 100-1)

12. INDICATING YOUR OWN INTENTION
    *Tegami-o kakoo-to omoimasu.* (I think I will write a letter.)

    It is awkward to say: *Tegami-o kaku-to omoimasu*, because it sounds as if you are talking about someone else.

Additional examples:
    *Undoo-o shiyoo-to omoimasu.* (I think I will exercise some.)

*Moo yameyoo-to omoimashita.* (I thought I would quit it then.)

(cf. IMJ, pp. 147, 150; NN-1, pp. 88-9)

13. *WAKARU* AND *SHIRU*

A: *Ashita doko-e ikimasu-ka.* (A: Where are you going tomorrow?)

B: *Mada wakarimasen.* (B: I don't know yet.)

It is wrong to say: *Mada shirimasen.* When referring to what you can decide for yourself, *wakarimasen* should be used.

(cf. NN-1, pp. 56-7)

14. TALKING ABOUT OTHER PEOPLE'S FEELINGS

a) *Tanaka-san-wa ureshisoo-desu.* (Mr. Tanaka looks happy.)

It is wrong to say: *Tanaka-san-wa ureshii-desu.*

Such adjectives as *ureshii, kanashii* (sad) and *sabishii* (lonely) are used for your own feeling when used alone.

Additional example:

*Kanashisoona kao-o shimashita.* (He looked sad. — *lit.* He made a sad looking face.)

(cf. IMJ, p. 146; NN-1, pp. 86-7)

b) *Tanaka-san-wa ureshii-deshoo.* (I think that Mr. Tanaka must be happy.)

You can express other people's feeling by adding *deshoo* to adjectives used for expressing your own feelings.

(cf. IMJ, p. 74; NN-2, pp. 72-3)

15. *IKU* AND *KURU*

A: *Koko-e kite-kudasai.* (A: Please come here.)

B: *Hai, ima ikimasu.* (B: Yes, I'm coming.)

It is wrong to say: *Ima kimasu. Kuru* is used when you refer to someone (including yourself) or something coming to where you are when you speak. Therefore you can say *Mata kimasu* (I'll come again) when referring to coming to the same place where you are now. But in the situation of the example

154

above, you are coming to where someone else is, so you can't use *kuru*.
Additional example:
*Ashita otaku-e ikimasu.* (I'll come to your house tomorrow.)
To be polite, *ukagaimasu, mairimasu, ojama-shimasu* are used in place of *ikimasu*.
(cf. NN-3, pp. 78-9)

16. *SORE* AND *ARE*; *SONO* AND *ANO*
*Kinoo Tanaka-san-to yuu hito-ni aimashita. Sono hito-wa kaishain-desu.* (I met a Mr. Tanaka yesterday. He works for a company.)
It is wrong to say: *Ano hito-wa kaishain-desu*, when the listener does not know Mr. Tanaka. *Ano* or *are* is used when the speaker and the listener share the same knowledge.
Additional example:
A: *Yamada-san-ga nyuuin-shimashita.* (A: Mr. Yamada has been hospitalized.)
B: *Soo-desu-ka. Sore-wa shirimasen-deshita.* (B: Is that right? I didn't know that.)
(cf. NN-1, pp.40-1)

17. ASKING FOR PERMISSION
*Moo kaette-mo ii-desu-ka.* (May I leave now?)
It is wrong to say: *Moo kaeru-koto-wa ii-desu-ka.*
: *Moo kaeru-(no)wa ii-desu-ka.*
Additional example:
*Tabako-o sutte-mo ii-desu-ka.* (May I smoke?)
*Deshoo-ka* is also used in place of *desu-ka*.
(cf. IMJ, p. 161)

18. EXPRESSING SUBSEQUENT ACTION
*Shokuji-o shite-kara dekakemasu.* (I will go out after I eat.)
It is wrong to say: *Shokuji-o shita-kara de-kakemasu*, because *kara* after the *ta* form means "because." Sometimes you will sound

155

wrong because of the pronunciation of the *te* sound; try hard to distinguish between *te* and *ta*, and between *de* and *da*.

Additional example:

*Ocha-o nonde-kara yarimashoo.* (Let's do it after we have had some tea.)

(cf. NN-1, p. 107)


19. PARTIAL NEGATION

*Zenbu-wa dekimasen-deshita.* (I couldn't do all of them.)

It is ambiguous to say: *Zenbu dekimasen-deshita.* This may mean "I couldn't do any of them."

Also,

*Zenbu dekita wake-ja arimasen.* (I couldn't do all.)

(cf. NN-3, pp. 56-7)


20. TAKING A TEST

*Shiken-o ukemashita.* (I took a test.)

It is wrong to say: *Shiken-o torimashita.*

: *Shiken-o moraimashita.*

(cf. NN-2, p. 67)


21. MAKING A REQUEST

*Tanaka-san-ni tanomimashita.* (I asked Mr. Tanaka to do it.)

It is wrong to say: *Tanaka-san-ni kikimashita*, which means "I asked Mr. Tanaka a question" or "I heard it from Mr. Tanaka."

(cf. IMJ, pp. 242, 256)


22. ASKING A QUESTION

*Tanaka-san-ni shitsumon-shimashita.* (I asked Mr. Tanaka a question.)

*Tanaka-san-ni kikimashita.*

*Tanaka-san-ni tazunemashita.*

It is wrong to say: *Tanaka-san-ni shitsumon-o kikimashita.*

(cf. IMJ, p. 79)

23. ASKING WISHES POLITELY
*Ocha(-wa) ikaga-desu-ka.* (Would you like some tea?)

It is impolite to say: *Ocha-o nomitai-desu-ka. . . . tai-desu-ka* is used with your equals, not to your superiors.

(cf. NN-1, pp. 12-3)


24. RECEIVING SOMETHING FROM SOME-ONE
*Otooto-ga kuremashita.* (My brother gave it to me.)
*Otooto-ni moraimashita.* (My brother gave it to me.)

It is wrong to say: *Otooto-ga watashi-ni agemashita.Ageru* is not used to refer to the speaker's receiving something.

To be humble:
*Tanaka-san-ni itadakimashita.* (Mr. Tanaka gave it to me.)
*Tanaka-san-ga kudasaimashita.* (Mr. Tanaka gave it to me.)

(cf. NN-2, pp. 128-9)


25. RECEIVING A FAVOR FROM SOMEONE
*Tanaka-san-ga tetsudatte-kuremashita.* (Mr. Tanaka helped me.)
*Tanaka-san-ni tetsudatte-moraimashita.* (Mr. Tanaka helped me.)

It is wrong to say: *Tanaka-san-ga tetsudai-o kuremashita.*

It is grammatically correct to say: *Tanaka-san-ga tetsudaimashita*, but this does not imply that you are grateful to Mr. Tanaka.

To be humble:
*Tanaka-san-ga tetsudatte-kudasaimashita.* (Mr. Tanaka helped me.)
*Tanaka-san-ni tetsudatte-itadakimashita.* (Mr. Tanaka helped me.)

(cf. NN-2, pp. 130-1)

# INDEX TO WORDS, PHRASES AND SENTENCES